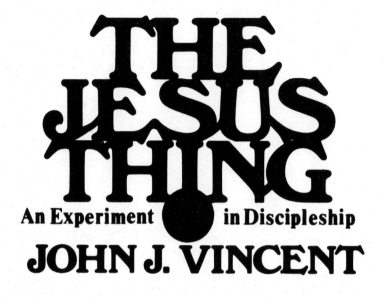

THE JESUS THING

An Experiment   in Discipleship

JOHN J. VINCENT

NASHVILLE   ABINGDON PRESS   NEW YORK

THE JESUS THING

Copyright © 1973 by Abingdon Press

Library of Congress Cataloging in Publication Data

Vincent, John J.
  The Jesus Thing.
  1. Christian life—1960-   2. Church renewal.
I. Title.
BV4501.2.V47   248'.4   73-322
ISBN 0-687-20221-3

MANUFACTURED BY THE PARTHENON PRESS AT
NASHVILLE, TENNESSEE, UNITED STATES OF AMERICA

To My Mother
and My Father

"Write a simple book
about things that are
really happening."

CONTENTS

LOOKING FOR SOMETHING

Can I commit my life to anything? Is there anything in human cultures as they exist today worth saving, worth committing my life to?

Margaret Mead, *Culture and Commitment.*

WHY PEOPLE ARE IN DESPAIR

A mood of quiet despair has settled over Christendom.

Church leaders still make noises. A conference, a new book, a chance meeting, the survival of old well-loved routines, the permanence of tested friends, the sound of words which formerly inspired—we keep going by whatever we can find that holds us. But nobody speaks about the future. Nobody any longer has great expectations. The debates in the churches do not mention Jesus.

Many magnificent people are still with it. "We just feel we have to keep coming." "It's a rough patch just now, but tomorrow may be different." "We come because of the children." "My friends are here."

But some magnificent people are no longer with it. There are numerous reasons—sociological, geographical, cultural, financial. There are many symptoms—disillusionment, disbelief, involvement in other things.

But one thing unites both groups: a feeling of faint but persisting unhappiness, disappointment. **There once was, after all, something about Jesus, which we learnt as children, which we sang about together, which we were told was the "most beautiful story of all." It still haunts us.** We do not know what to do

© Pierce & Washabaugh

with it. The church cannot help, for she evidently does not know what do with it either.

And there are new generations, growing up into this scene of quiet despair. They look around, they look at us, they feel our despair, and they go and look somewhere else. They are not hostile; but they are sad.

A year or so ago, a group of us thought it would be worthwhile arranging a series of residential weekend conferences in various parts of England, designed to get together young adults—

people in their late teens and twenties—under the theme, "Looking for Something." So far, we have had four. At the second session of every conference, we talk about "What Are We Looking For?"

It is always initially a grueling experience. Time and time again I have found that people cannot get on to what they want to say until they have got the past out of their hair. In fact, they can at first only see the new, the radical, or the different, as something over against and different from what they have known in the past.

So, in word or occasionally on paper, they list "Why the church as it is drives me up the wall," or "makes me a radical," or "frustrates me, bruises me, bores me."

Many people in the churches, and not least in the churches' leadership, need to hear this. They still do not see why this generation has produced a whole crop of radicals. They do not see why there is any need radically to change. And many church members, not all of them over 40 (though many are), need to hear it. For they, too, still think that things can be improved by patient tinkering which leaves the basics untouched.

Let us set down some typical answers to the question about frustration in the church:

1) because its work at present has ceased to have any meaning for the majority of people, who see no point in raising money to keep going outdated buildings and traditions.

2) because the church too often plays no real part in the life of the community around it, and its members are not involved as Christians in community life.

3) because the church's services and meetings are too often treated as a separate part of churchgoers' lives—their church life and secular life stand apart from, and are almost irrelevant to, each other.

4) because the church's actions are often a violation of Christian principles and values.

5) because the church does not express in its actions the influence, dynamic, and actions of a risen Christ who is concerned with all people in all situations.

6) because the church does not have time to help where needed, because it is so busy looking after itself.

7) because the church has become part of the establishment, and always opposes progress and those who wish to change things.

A particular area of frustration for people in their twenties is the worship and fellowship of the local church. Thus people who want to be Christians are endlessly thwarted in their efforts to discover meaningful or authentic ways in which they may encounter the faith within the churches. Typical comments are:

1) the worship of the church is not relevant to my way of life and thought. **I don't understand the hymns and the out-of-date language, and do not see why I should have to.**

photo by Richard Lee

2) there is little or no thinking going on—yet many thinking people are in the church.

3) even if the services were to be treated as a retreat from the outside world and a source of strength, etc., they are too dull and stereotyped to play this role for me.

4) the architecture, music, decorations, and dress associated with churches is nineteenth-century or earlier.

5) sermons say the same thing every week, and preachers are poorly informed of thinking and events in the world. The intellectual level is far below that of the contemporary counterparts—the T.V. documentary, political speech, average lecture.

6) there is too little emphasis on discussion—people listen but fall into the role of passive listeners, which leads to stagnation. They need to be stirred up, made to think about where they stand. At the moment, a conservative sort of faith is taken for granted.

Inevitably, many today object to the churches as institutions. Typical comments are:

1) the church as an institution has very little idea of its function in the modern world.

2) **the church wields authority it should not possess, and is based on a hierarchical structure which denies the spirit of Jesus.**

3) people who get mixed up in the church end up simply serving an institution which exercises more and more control over them, and they often cease to remember its true purpose.

4) too much is decided at the top. There is no personal involvement and responsibility in important decisions.

5) the institution's life constantly avoids necessary discussion of what Christianity is really about.

6) because of absence of trained and competent employees, there is constant inefficiency, waste of money, and confusion.

7) **the church is a middle-class institution.** The full churches

are always in socially good areas. Minorities and poor people are ignored.

Often it is church people who are the stumbling block in the way of people becoming involved in the churches. A few among many reasons given are:

1) bickering among congregations.

2) lack of feeling of community.

3) lack of concern by individuals.

4) hostility to youth.

5) hypocrisy and unchristian attitudes.

6) when it comes to the crunch, Christians back up their own economic interests, and thus do nothing about South Africa, or unjust wages, or bad conditions.

7) members of churches behave exactly as do members of any other human organization—their behavior is adequately described in psychological, sociological, and behavioral terms, without the necessity for any doctrines of grace, forgiveness, prayer, providence, or "spiritual things."

8) Whether or not someone becomes involved in helping others, or in community concerns, or in political or social action, depends upon their native disposition, not upon whether or not they are members of churches.

THEOLOGICAL OBJECTIONS

Many of the objections raised by young adults against current practices are objections to the theological presuppositions and teachings of the churches today. Typical are:

1) Christianity has tried to teach the principle of God as a figure to look up to and to obey, rather than as a spiritual force which guides one in all one does.

2) Such theology as is expressed within the church seems either woolly to the extent of degenerating into sentimentalism or depends upon people feeling "sinners" before they can make contact with Jesus.

3) There is embarrassingly oversimple theological phraseology, like "God loves you, God cares for you, God is watching your every action," etc. Unacceptable (to me) theological beliefs are accepted as the norm, and criticism of these condemns you automatically as being either unchristian or wavering (e.g., virgin birth).

4) The theology behind everything that goes on (a) assumes that people still believe in a literal heaven and hell, and (b) assumes we should be "saved" and then should be "happy," "have assurance." Whereas, in fact (a) people do not actually *believe* or *experience* all this, (b) people experience totally other facts of Christian existence for which the old theology is not descriptive.

5) There is a stress on certainty—"we know"—rather than a

church being the place where doubts are expressed and shared. **Instead of "modern day problems" and "Christian answers," the central focal point is always the Bible, which is not where people begin their thinking today.**

6) The set of beliefs held by the church today is regarded as complete and immutable, whereas I believe that truth is being constantly revealed, and that these revelations are being ignored—particularly at the local level.

Naturally, the theological views of people in and around their twenties have been affected by the theological debates of our time, or by the slogans issuing from them. Often, from school friends, teachers, or other adults, more or less radical views have been accepted which remain alongside conservative church ideas to which they otherwise adhere. The general result is complete confusion—or the conclusion that theology is used merely to justify established habits, conservative or progressive.

One element is constant and outstanding: the conviction that the theology of the churches is something quite different from the teaching of Jesus. Jesus' words and deeds have problems, but the problems of relating them to the views of the churches are infinitely greater. Naturally, there is an element of "generation gap" between young adults and the churches as a whole. But the young adult feels he has Jesus "on his side" precisely here, as over against the authoritarian theology of the churches.

At the same time, there is also little expectation that any "sense" can be made of the Jesus story, which would make any difference to contemporary life. The Sermon on the Mount, the Beatitudes, the Parable of the Good Samaritan, and the Story of the Rich Young Ruler (the passages most popularly recalled) are felt to have been more or less ignored by the churches in their teachings and life. But there is no great hope that they could be applied to life in a different way. Apart from the general command to "love your neighbor as yourself," the teachings of Jesus are not felt to be of much practical value, despite being "a great ideal," or "the way men should live." Jesus is seen as little less of a problem to practical life than to the churches, however much people may not want to "ditch him altogether."

WHY WE ARE STILL IN IT

After listing the reasons which young adults have for objecting to current church belief and practice, we ask another question:
Why, given all this, are you still in the church?
The answers are revealing. Sometimes it is obvious that people have not yet marked out why they remain within the church; they are simply hanging on, hoping that something will turn up. In answer to the question "Why are you still in the church?" one answers, "Because the minister says he'll get his big stick out if I'm not there, so I go once a month to please him." Another writes, "Because that's where everyone else is, who thinks it ought to be blown up."

More serious comments divide into those which focus on a justification, despite everything, of some form of institutional Christianity, and those which focus on personal reasons which keep Christians within churches of which they otherwise disapprove. Among personal reasons are:

1) Because I draw from it my spiritual needs necessary in liv-

ing; I don't find life totally satisfying unless I've had contact with Christian people.

2) **Because I still believe in shared worship and find the symbolism behind Holy Communion meaningful.**

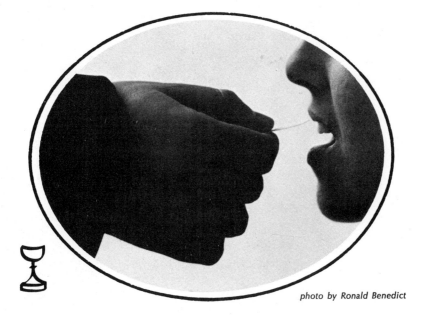

photo by Ronald Benedict

3) Because my church does some good for the community, I feel that I should associate with this.

4) Because I think that Christ has some meaning to the world, and some people in the church are concerned with this.

5) Because there is no other group of people whose sole and specific task is to carry on the words, deeds, and traditions of Jesus, which to me are the meaning of life.

6) Because whatever shambles the church might be at the moment, its members do profess to be followers of Jesus. His life and words do seem to be relevant to every age, and form for me a pattern by which to live out my life.

The second group of reasons focus upon the "institutional" aspects of the churches. People "stay in":

photo by Ronald Benedict

1) **Because, in spite of all the faults, the church is made up of individual Christians, and therefore needs reform from inside rather than from outside.** Some structures and institution is necessary for its effective life.

2) Because I think that there is a fair chance that it can be changed (to something better) in an economic way rather than to let it die or bulldoze it before starting a new church.

3) Because the church still has resources, both human and financial, which could be used to develop a more dynamic, more universal, more radical approach to Christianity.

4) Because the new church, the radical church, the revolutionary or liberated church, needs to be asserted as a proper, or *the* proper, church, and this can be done only when it is within the old church as well as alongside it. The consequent tensions will create a situation for growth and progressive change.

Perhaps I should add a personal comment on the question of whether or not to stay in the churches as they are.

I think I see it as fundamentally a question of responsibility for others. Obviously, anyone is free to leave at any time. But most of those around whom this book is written do in fact keep in touch with churches, either seriously or casually, either in hope or in despair. They do so, I think, more or less as I do—because you do not do everything that you are free to do. "All things are lawful, but not all things are expedient," as Paul says in I Cor. 6:12. "Expedient" can only mean "useful to other people." I believe it is more useful to the churches that people like us should remain visibly within them; and more useful to others like us that we should be visibly committed to the first mile of conventional church adherence as well as to the second mile of radical church creation.

WHAT I LIVE BY

Radical Christians have large criticisms of the church. Yet many still remain, with varying degrees of commitment, within the church. And the question arises: what kind of church would make sense from the radical Christian point of view?

Radical Christians have also large criticisms of the beliefs and practices of other contemporary Christians. Yet they still remain convinced that they are, and must call themselves, Christians. The question thus arises: what kind of faith is it by which the radical Christian lives?

This is a "confessional" question in two senses. In the first sense, it is a question about everyman's private existence, about how he sees things, about "what makes him tick," about how he thinks of himself as a man in the world who is called by Christ and discipled to him. So that the "Looking for Something" conferences asked their members to set down "What I Live By." These are a few of the results, which naturally range from the somewhat cynical to the more searching, from the simple to the more complicated.

1) **I live by the rat-race of material possessions—but I try to escape from it, and therefore I think I ought to support the Christian type of things sometimes. I believe the Christian life would work in the world.**

photo by Ronald Benedict

2) I try to live by maximum availability for service to others consistent with a fair degree of self-interest.

3) I live by a search for happiness, and I seem to find this in many spheres of life. But amid this search, the basic simplicity of Christ's teachings and actions stands out and, put into practice, gives me contentment. I find that being within a community, i.e., in fellowship in it, gives me the greatest happiness or "blessedness."

4) I live by a simple everyday faith—that God through Christ will sustain us. "Be content with the things of today: tomorrow will take care of itself."

5) **I live by a group who have this Christ thing in their guts and who are acting out this thing, which may or may not need vast machinery.** In practice it's the difficult job of trying to enrich

photo by Steve Sparks

everything around this group in a way which justifies its claim that this Christ thing is the ultimate way of life for man.

6) I live by a view of existence, which to me is what Jesus stands for, which involves a new total attitude to life and people based on the assumption that the dynamics of the Kingdom are at work in all men, all things, and all history.

7) I live by doing the Jesus thing, helping the poor, feeding the hungry, etc., in whatever way is appropriate to the present day. This also means that I must help make others believe in the gospel of love, so I am also concerned about evangelism and even *numbers* in the church.

8) **I live by a belief that I am here to improve the physical side of the earth as well as the social.** I want to become one of

photo by Ronald Benedict

the people who helps to conquer the environment for the material good of all men. I think that there are things I should do because I am a Christian as well as things I should do in a Christian way.

9) I live by faith, that is, by doing things for which there is no immediate justification; by hope, that is, by expecting that, despite history, there is always a pay-off for what is right, or generous, or imaginative, or liberating, or healing; and by love, that is, by the upsurge of humanity in the human heart which is grace.

At the end of one conference, we formed up groups to prepare "A Tentative Creed of the Faith We Actually Hold," and the result points already to some of the "lines" which will emerge later:

"We believe that the Jesus story gives meaning to all life. We therefore have an understanding of life based on the faith that the things of Jesus, such as

healing the sick,

feeding the hungry,

giving people hints of the love of God,

are the beginning and ending of all things.

"We believe that we are now Jesus, and the Jesus people. We believe that we must carry on his work. This means:

1) that we are committed totally to his way as our way;

2) that we must give our lives in *service* of the Kingdom;

3) that we must *reach* to others to show them what is happening in life.

"We believe that this requires a total *commitment,* some of the elements of which seem to us immediately to comprise challenges and calls to us. We believe, then,

1) that we are called to *work,* and that the work we do is our Christian vocation—and therefore some of us must *change our jobs.*

2) that we are called to *self-denial,* and that the money we have is for others—and therefore some of us must *change our situation in life.*

3) that we are called to a *new community*, and that new homes, houses, groups are needed—and therefore some of us must *move house.*

4) that we are part of a *revolutionary life-style*, and that new ways of embodying acceptance, love, liberation, sympathy are needed—and therefore all of us must *be liberated* from some bourgeois, family, or ecclesiastical expectations."

Thus, the conferences ended very practically. In some cases, people who attended became committed to different jobs. Several of them reappear in Part Four, as members of the experimental Ashram Community.

But, just as important, the faith that was being expressed as a result of these conferences was clearly something rather different from the theology and assumptions of the churches, which the groups largely rejected. Therefore, we were constantly faced with the *fact* of a different kind of faith, actually being produced by people when they together considered important issues affecting their own real lives and the lives of others. There was an implicit "new beginning" already, in the way the Christian faith was actually working for some of these people. And, further, there was a tentative but insistent demand that theology and life make more of Jesus than the churches had made. These are the clues which I want to try to follow in the next two parts of the book.

NEW BEGINNINGS

THE SECRET

Suppose, for example, that a man, or a number of people, had discovered a great secret which they wished to disclose to others.
. . . It's a matter of passing on a secret, and solely to those who are ready to receive it. Once is enough. Obviously, this restricts the circulation, and slows down the tempo. But why should we be in a hurry? The person aflame with awareness and desire who is already on the edge of the secret will know how to find us, and he will not need any lengthy exposition. A single word will be enough to enlighten him, a single action, a gesture, a look, a smile, a silence. . . . And then you have a man who is no longer alone, or lost, or astray, or defenseless, or crushed by the State.

Petru Dimitriu, *Incognito*.

SOMETHING NEW IS HAPPENING

"It's all happening!"

A group of us, a couple of years ago, were meeting in Ashram Community House in Rochdale. One had recently been accepted for training in social work. Another had just been accepted as a candidate for the ministry. Another had refused to take degree finals, as that would mean complicity in a system she thought evil. Another was busy being bloodied by the church establishment. Another was debating what job he could do, in middle life, now that he was free of family ties. Another was debating the relative merits of whole time, part time, and spare time fulfillment of what she knew she really ought to be doing.

"Yes. It's all happening, *just as he said,*" joined in one of them.

"Yes," said another. "And the tragedy is that, to us, what's happening *is* the Jesus story. But the churches just don't see it, or don't appear to. They go on doing the same old irrelevant things, while the real church isn't there at all."

"That's it. There's a new church. Around the Jesus thing."

"And that, John, is what you must call the book you're writing. And it must be about *action,* and how action undergirds theology, and is undergirded by it."

So here is the book. And if I had to say why I venture to add yet another to the rows of recent books on Christianity, I'd just have to say, in all naïvety, that I don't seem to have heard it said quite the way I hear a lot of people saying it now, and quite the way I've learnt to say it. I would have to say that almost all the books on the church which came out of the renewal theologies of the 1960s were deficient so far as *the future* was concerned.[1] They were dependent upon particular theological viewpoints—often a combination of Paul Tillich with reigning sociology. But even more, they were obliged to be long on theory and short on action.

Now, we have seen some of the weaknesses of the kind of church operation which the renewal theologies undermined. I do not think that this means an end to "renewal" itself within established churches. But the renewal has not been thorough, or fast, or long-lasting enough. And it has now been overtaken by other factors, of which I would name six.

1. *The Rise of the New Liberation Consciousness.* This has come to affect the thinking of many younger Christians only over the past three or four years, and only now is beginning to affect church theology—though no one quite knows what to do with it.[2] **We need now to see what this new way of thinking has to contribute to faith and to church life.** We need not to "take it into

---

[1] An excellent example—and summary—is R. G. Jones and A. J. Wesson, *Towards a Radical Church* (London: Epworth Press, 1970).

[2] Probably the best-known example of the new left, radical Christian is the slightly eccentric, mainly catholic, monthly *Roadrunner* (28 Brundretts Road, Manchester 21).

our system," which would smother it, but rather to leave room for it.

2. *The Emergence of New Experimental Groups in Britain.* The groups I have in mind all appeared in the last three or four years. They came after or alongside the renewal experiments, which mainly in fact extended or changed local congregations. **The new groups are more hybrid, more self-conscious in their effort to create new styles which will be meaningful to their memberships, more insistent that new forms must grow from the bottom up, and not be imposed as pieces of renewal from the top.**[3] Perhaps the tragedy of the short-lived non-church move-

photo by Sid Dorris

ment [4] highlights again the absolute necessity for such experimental groups to persevere with styles which avoid running out into the sand.

3. *The Hardening of the Establishments.* In all the denominations, the renewal "spring" of the mid 1960s has passed quickly to the autumn of distrust, of "rationalizing our experiments" (which can mean rubbing them out), of "maintaining our traditional work" (which can mean abandoning nontraditional work), of

[3] A newsletter is at present lacking, but perhaps the need will be met by the "One for Christian Renewal" Bulletin (c/o Publishing Services Partnership, 82 High Road, London, N2 9PW).

[4] See Ray Billington, *The Christian Outsider* (London: Epworth Press, 1971).

"not embarrassing the authorities" (which can mean leaving them running the whole show). **Councils of churches, local and national, have also tended to withdraw from enterprises which cause trouble.**[5] The money is running short—for the World Council

of Churches, the British Council of Churches, for the denominations. Soon, only the old endowed ecclesiastical mausoleums will remain!

[5] Cf. Paul R. Clifford, *Now Is the Time* (London: Lutterworth Press, 1971). Also various reports of the British Council of Churches: *Together for the Seventies* (1969); *Local Councils of Churches Today* (1971); *Ecumenical Experiments: a Handbook*, by R. M. C. Jeffrey, 1971 (all from British Council of Churches, 10, Eaton Gate, London S.W.1).

photo by Ronald Benedict

4. *Disillusion with the Theological Debates.* **The theological reductionism of the 1960s seems to be at an end, and many of the positions which excited us then now look rather thin.**[6] Few people are interested any more in being intellectually "honest to God," or in arguing about rival positions. The traditional theologies can be left in their graves. The radical theologies will be heard only if they create radical life-styles. As Lawrence Bright says, "The new theology . . . is untrue to itself unless it can be verified within the history made by those who profess it." [7] It is a tall order, but a justified one.

[6] Alistair Kee, *The Way of Transcendence* (London: Pelican Books, 1971).
[7] Lawrence Bright, "The Future of Renewal," *Christian Renewal,* 2 (June, 1971), p. 7. This quarterly is a very useful forum for catholic and other renewal interests (*Christian Renewal,* 11, Broomfield Road, Henfield, Sussex).

photo by Ronald Benedict

5. *A Revival of Interest in Jesus.* **Alongside disillusionment with academic theology, there is also a new fascination with Jesus.** In some, it is the Jesus of *Superstar* or *Godspell*, or the Pentecostal revival, or the Jesus freaks. But others see Jesus as the key to a radical life-style, see theology as "Christology and dis-

cipleship." I believe that this revival of interest in Jesus will ultimately be the way of raising the God question again in new ways.[8] At any rate, this present book is very much about those who are content to stay with a few Christ-centered insights for a decade, to get on with discovering what clues there are to life and all things in "the Jesus thing."

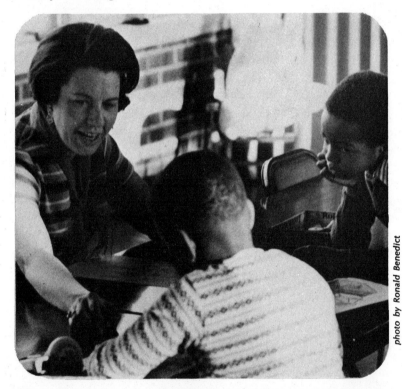

photo by Ronald Benedict

6. *Action as Devotion*. **Allied to this rediscovery of Jesus has come a new concern with radical politics, and the concentration of effort upon various contemporary issues which seemed at once to be related to Jesus, but which were unrelated to the churches.** War, race, investment policy, economic injustice, pollution, population crisis and urban community problems are all

[8] Cf. the volume of essays: *New Soundings: Towards a Christ-Centered Radicalism*, ed. John J. Vincent (forthcoming).

closely connected.[9] Each have produced their own radical Christian responses all over the world. The British ones await a commentary: the American ones have been more widely recorded.[10]

Such, then, are elements in the "something new" which is happening. From this time on, I shall assume this situation as the backdrop for what I shall write—and, in the main, avoid further footnotes.

What follows is my own personal response to this situation.

Inevitably, it is tied to a particular piece of my own life. For thirteen years, I had been a city mission minister, in Manchester and in Rochdale. Finally, despairing of finding time ever to do concentrated theological work, I'd taken off a year, to teach theology in Boston and in New York. It proved to be a year of personal stocktaking (at forty it was perhaps not a bad year for that!). The year fortified me in my conviction that, for a time at least, some of the things that had to be thought and done, were best thought and done in experimental situations. Hence, my engagement with Urban Theology Unit [11] and the Ashram community, which represented a decision to take a few years to go back to the grass roots, back to Jesus, back to the people, both young and my own contemporaries, who were quietly but persistently demanding and experimenting with new forms of faith and commitment, and new ways of putting a roof over them.

A NEW CHRISTIANITY?

The call for new theological thinking and action thus comes from the growing number of disillusioned radicals still in, or recently having left, the church.

The group which can loosely be called the "radical Christians"

[9] Cf., e.g., John J. Vincent, *The Race Race* (London: S.C.M. Press, 1971).

[10] John Pairman Brown, *The Liberated Zone: A Guide to Christian Resistance* (Richmond, Va.: John Knox Press, 1971).

[11] See the tri-annual journal, *New City* (Urban Theology Unit, 233 Abbeyfield Road, Sheffield S4 7AW, from where details of courses, study weeks, research projects, etc. are also available).

manifests itself in innumerable forms, some of them odd, some of them outwardly rather conventional. The kind of radical Christians I most frequently meet are those from all the churches, mainly in the 20-45 age range, who have come through the theological experiments of the 1960s, and more or less take for granted the negative position resulting from them. They no longer find it necessary to argue that most of the God they grew up on is dead, that 95 percent of the institutional churches are variously irrelevant, evil, or hostile, and that there is now no necessity for any more literature. conferences, or groups to underline these facts. The net result of the decade is that, for a whole generation, every door which had seemed to be open in 1960 is now seen to be closed, every attempt prematurely to rehabilitate traditional theologies or philosophies is now seen to be illegitimate, and every easy answer to the radical Christians' dilemma is seen to be ill conceived.

In this situation, many have become ex-Christians, and even more ex-churchpeople. All over America and Britain, people are gathering together who used to belong to churches, sometimes to talk over the possibility of a relevant form of Christianity for today and tomorrow, more often to engage in practical work in the community or in dealing with world problems, such as race or poverty. It may well be that a whole generation or more will have to pass before these persons are able again to relate to those who still retain membership of traditional churches. But it is vital that the personal links should be sustained and strengthened.

In this situation, three things are vitally necessary. First, *some of us must give ourselves to the para-church now emerging.* Some of us still within the structures must stand also with those who cannot remain there. We must patiently work with them in the construction of new forms of the church, built around specific deeds of Christ in the world, or around specific groups of individuals with distinctive interests, or around particular ethnic, geographical, vocational, and even theological groupings. The parachurch has already begun to appear, not based on sentimental nostalgia (like the underground church), but based on more radical commitment than the structured church, and a determination to face squarely the obligation to create a total Christian ministry of a new kind, in a totally different situation. Happily, the para-church does not always need to stand alone, as there are also growing numbers of ecumenical groups, action churches, and renewed congregations which can at times assist it.

But a second item is equally important. The para-church, the ecumenical groups, and the action churches *are in danger of disappearing for lack of sufficient theological oxygen.* The denominations continue their peculiar inheritances, the theologians continue their erudite discussions, the ecumaniacs continue to find a similar non-faith or post-faith in all the churches. **But the radicals, jostled from secularity to death of God, from Jesusology to sociology, are in danger of having nothing really to live by.**

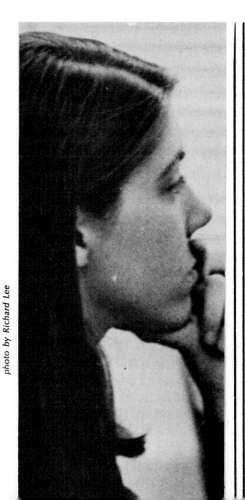

photo by Richard Lee

In the old church, it did not show too much that no one took the theology seriously. But in the radical church or the para-church, the only thing you have to go on is theology, for everything goes straight from theology to action. And radicalism just has not produced a total faith yet. Perhaps it is too early. But this book at any rate makes one attempt to create a new theology for the radicals, based on the assumption that people only want any sort of church at all if they are still in some way hooked on Jesus, and based on the further assumption that the Jesus faith to which the churches are still officially attached simply does not fill the bill.

So, can the radical Christians move from talking to living? Or, more crucially, is there anything in the Jesus story which might suggest lines for the new Christianity, which will sustain and propel and judge the new Christians, in a time in which the rules, regulations, worship, and fellowship of the old churches just cannot do this any more (even though many, like myself, will continue to support them for the sake of those to whom they are meaningful)?

Of course, this is an "insider's" question. It is not the question of people outside the Jesus group. I think they might be a bit more interested in some radical answers than they are likely to be in the traditional ones. But let us not deceive ourselves. **We are writing and talking and fighting for the diminishing number of people who are still prepared for the possibility that there is something in the Jesus Story, and thus in Christianity, different from what Christendom or the churches have made of it, but nevertheless still tied very much to that enigmatic, impossible revolutionary of Nazareth.** That is the stance I write from. And I write for others who have that stance—who are neither with the middle-aged who have settled for establishment religion, nor with the young who have settled for nothing. They are those who cannot abide the Jesus of the churches, yet who cannot throw Jesus aside.

What that group does for itself, for its children, and for the whole church is perhaps even more important than what the middle-aged do with church unity, or what the young do with

Zen or pot or sex. Or, at least, it is *as* important. And I do not need to be told that there are many radicals in middle age and youth who will share the search, or that many in my generation will find it all ridiculous or misguided!

Third, *theology must follow action.* **So long as it is a matter of jumping on some new intellectual bandwagon, theology is dead.** It is dead not because God is dead, but because there are

From A Porcine History of Philosophy and Religion *by James Taylor.* © *1972 by Abingdon Press.*

SITUATION ETHICS PIG AND PRINCIPLES ETHICS PIG DISCUSSING THE NATURE OF CHRISTIAN LOVE

no God actions or God deeds around raising the question of God. There only needs to be thinking, systematizing, when there is something to systematize.

Ideally, of course, the whole of life, life in all its humanness, should raise the God question. In a sense, it does. But the God question which is merely the question arising from man's contemporary existence in Western affluence in the nineteen-seventies is still the question simply of man in his own airtight compartment. His life there certainly raises questions which some people at some times have called or even will call God questions. But it is not the whole of Christian theology. Even more important: although it is the place to start, it is not *what you say*. It is the context, not the content. It is the situation, not the message. It is God's yes to man, but not yet God's action in man. It is man's agenda, but not yet what the Christian has to bring to it.

© 1967 Abingdon Press

So theology should be pushed along by action, not action by theology. It was so with the Jesus story. Theology arose as a necessity because of the new happenings of Jesus and his disciples. Theology arose as a reflection upon the Jesus events, as a comment upon the Jesus deeds, as the human attempt to make sense of something which had happened. Constantly in the Gospels, an action of Jesus precipitates controversy, and controversy precipitates a question, and the question causes Jesus' teaching. The church today reverses it all: much teaching but no questions, because no controversy, because no action!

Today it can hardly be as easy as in the Gospels. Too much of the church's action is geared to the past, is merely continuing the traditions. So that for us today, another element must be added

to the definition that theology follows action. It is this: **Theology awaits Jesus action.** That is, just as the stuff of Christian theology in the beginning was the Jesus action, so the stuff of a new Christian theology today must be Jesus action.

What is Jesus action? The main purpose of this book is to attempt to describe it. But we had to try to establish that it *was* the business of Christians in the first place. And we had to say why it wasn't so simple a matter as might at first sight appear.

So, our task becomes clearer. It is to answer two questions: Is there action in the para-church or the institutional church which assumes a theology not yet explicit? And is there a theology emerging which can make sense of current moods and actions in ways impossible to traditional theologies?

THE BREAD THAT'S RISING

The liberated church will cease to be liberated as soon as it succumbs to the temptation to start ordering its doctrines, beliefs, and disciplines. Thus in the past, every reformation, movement, vocation, or operation became ossified. Precisely so developed the oppressive sects of our time, from Roman Catholicism to Methodism, from Pentecostalism to Greek Orthodoxy. The liberated church exists now within all these, and more. To "organize" it will be to kill it. But, in the words of the Emmaus House (in New York) occasional magazine, *The Bread Is Rising*. New yeast is swelling in the Christian camp. It isn't so much a matter of listing "distinctive doctrines"—we have had enough of that in the existing churches—but rather of "characteristic attitudes." They will be found in varying degrees elsewhere. But they exist sufficiently within contemporary groups of Christians to justify some attempt to depict some leading lines and assumptions.

Later, we will consider the implications of these lines and assumptions so far as the old and new churches' structures are concerned. Initially, we depict a "life style."

1. The Liberated Church Is Fundamentally People in Revolt. Theodore Roszak calls his attractive but not uncritical report on the new liberation consciousness in America, *The Making of a Counter Culture*.[1] Given the technocratic society, it is inevitable that the main lines of that culture should produce their opposites in the young and the radicals. So far as Christians are concerned, there is thus a double problem. On the one side, Christians see as keenly as their secular and humanist and Marxist friends the evils of the technocratic society. But they see also that many of the characteristics of that society—acquisitiveness, pride in possessions, conservatism, intolerance, insensitivity to persons, anxiety to solve personal issues by managerial methods, subservience of individuals to doctrines and schemes, preference for "returns" over authenticity, concern for public image over honesty—are characteristics of the churches as they see them today.

Add to this the decisive third element—that Jesus is seen as also "against" the assumptions of technocratic society and thus against the churches which reflect them, and it can only be expected that the first response will be one of revolt.

2. *The Liberated Church Is Fundamentally People Seeking Dis-*

[1] Theodore Roszak, *The Making of a Counter Culture* (New York: Bantam Books, 1970).

cipleship. The people I am talking about are not interested in the church for its own sake, but only as a means for continuing the "Jesus thing," and thus of being a force for change in the world, and of support for those engaged in change.

Thus, they see Christian obedience as something which must occur "from the bottom up." It must arise out of the dynamic created by the deeds of Christ, the needs of the world, and their own existence. Such obedience cannot be laid on by any church authority, or specified in any "obligations of church membership." It must arise in the clash of existence itself, where Christ, world, and personal being come to the flash point of decision. Only in that situation can one talk of commitment. Commitment cannot be made to vague principles, or creeds, or to churches as such. Commitment can be made only to specific deeds, to specific dynamic notions, to specific pieces of what churches might want or ask for. **Insofar as the churches require "carte blanche" commitment to whatever they might want—which in practice always means whatever the older members want of the younger ones! —they are seen as the antichrist.** That is, they are seen as the

Pledge Card

ESTIMATE OF GIVING

In grateful recognition that all my time, treasure, and ability come from God, I gladly join with others in the support of Christ's church.

AMOUNT PER WEEK

$____.⁰⁰ for local needs including worship, education, pastoral service, church care and upkeep, and the world outreach of the church through World Service and Conference Benevolences.

I prefer to use another plan, and will give as follows:

$____ per ____

SIGNATURE

____, 19 73

DATE

enemies of Jesus who calls men to free and responsible service, and thus liberates them from every other claim.

As one who has tried to study the Gospels' teaching on discipleship for many years, I can only say that I believe such attitudes are confirmed by the Gospel evidence.

The liberated church's concern is shared by many today. Toward the end of its life, *New Christian* concluded:

May it not be that the real work waiting to be initiated involves penetration beneath the surface of church and social reform to the source of renewal, namely a deeper commitment to Christ? Daily it becomes more apparent that the real malady afflicting the Church is not theological or structural archaism—these are only symptoms—but the lack of personal individual commitment to him who is the source of its life and the goal of all its striving. Until there is a renewal of commitment, it seems impossible for the shape of the Church's corporate life or the quality of its witness to be radically changed.[2]

The trouble is that such appeals have so often fallen on deaf ears or else have been used merely to get people more committed to the traditional loyalties. The liberated church seeks to take it seriously in terms of action, experiment and obedience to what are seen as the present implications of Jesus' work.

3. *The Liberated Church Is a Search for True Humanness.* "Humanness, please, not humanism," as Joseph Mathews of Chicago pleads. He is right. Humanism is a beautiful, logical assertion of the primacy and sufficiency of humanity. "Humanness" is more open-ended, a quality of being, an assertion of man's true nature, a reminder of what he essentially is, or could be.

Here, Jesus emerges again as "the proper man," whose style of operation, approach to others, inward self-authenticity, openness to circumstances, preparedness to be "used," and loyalty to what he sees to be God's will, become not so much a set of characteristics to be "imitated" as a living dynamic to become part of. Again, this style of Jesus' humanness was not achieved "for its own sake," in

[2] *New Christian*, January 21, 1970.

the way that piety or perfection used to be regarded as ends in themselves. Rather, it was achieved as a secondary result of his own service of the Kingdom of God. Jesus "learned obedience through the things he suffered." But, equally, he suffered only because of his faithful fulfillment of the deeds of the new Kingdom. Suffering is only a secondary aspect of christocentric humanness—it applies only when the Jesus deeds are rejected.

Thus, there is a degree of simplicity, of naïvety, of straightforwardness, of undesigning, about the liberated churchperson. In New Testament terms, he is "hid with Christ," but not in a devotional or ascetic or mystical sense, but in terms of the dynamics which inform his actions, life-style, and assumptions. Thus, he cannot avoid some affinity with the hippies—at least, he sees *why* they are what they are, and how significant their longing for humanity and simplicity are—and how nearly Christian. Jesus is the model for many of them; and those who have long worshiped their own version of a "gentle Jesus, meek and mild" can hardly object if hippies take him as the type of nonviolence, sim-

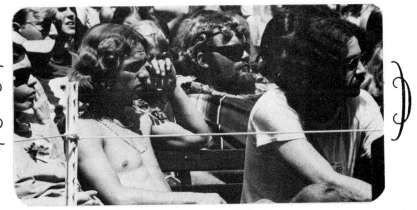

photo by Bracey Holt

plicity, nonpossession of goods, and communal living. **The hippies, however, are the extremists, the "way out," among the liberated, corresponding perhaps to the "over-converted" (Henry J. Cadbury) in the early church.** The liberated church shares their feelings to some extent, though not their way of life, however much it applauds their search for true humanness.

WHY "THE JESUS THING"?

Why the Jesus *thing?*

Partly because every other word is lost, or dead, or too linked with views we do not hold.

"Thing" can be taken as synonymous for the vast number of circumlocutions which the New Testament employs to describe that to which Jesus points, or that which Jesus embodies. In Mark it is "the Kingdom of God," in Matthew "the Kingdom of Heaven," in John "ageless life," in Acts "the gospel," in Paul "salvation," in the epistles of John "love." But every term that is employed is deficient. For it points beyond itself. The word is not the thing that the word tries to describe. The thing that the word tries to describe is "all that Jesus began to teach and do." The thing is the whole reality. It is too great for any word. So we settle for "thing."

"Thing" thus refers to a way or style which is fluid, imprecise, undogmatic. It is the predicate for everything for which "Jesus" is the subject. At a time of revolt against institutions, dogmas, creeds, and statements of belief, "the Jesus thing" may represent a spirit, a movement, a way, which refuses to be a blueprint for the future, but is satisfied to be a way of holding the gospel for us today.

Of course, "the Jesus Thing" is not a New Testament phrase. But it could be argued that it is a contemporary equivalent for "Kingdom," or "love," or "gospel." Actually, the New Testament itself comes near to using the phrase "the Jesus thing." Acts 18:25 speaks of "the things of (or concerning) Jesus." "The things of the Kingdom of God" occurs at Acts 1:3, and 19:8. The book of Acts ends at 28:31 with the phrase, "preaching the Kingdom of God, and teaching the things concerning the Lord Jesus Christ." The Greek is literally "the about the Lord Jesus Christ things," "all that pertains to the Lord Jesus Christ," "the Jesus Christ things."

There is another reason for preferring "the Jesus thing." It has been my complaint that so many approaches to Jesus take only one element and overemphasize it. I could happily speak of "the Jesus "presence" (incarnation), "the Jesus action" (healing), "the Jesus insight" (parables), "the Jesus style" (acted parables), "the Jesus groups" (disciples), "the Jesus cross" (self-sacrifice), "the Jesus spirit" (resurrection), and "the Jesus destiny" (parousia). But each overemphasizes one aspect. And it is the *total* reality pointed to and lived out by Jesus that I feel is important. Precisely this emphasis upon the totality of "what is Christ's" was achieved by the New Testament "things of Jesus Christ."

How, then, can we define "the Jesus thing"?

First, we cannot define it at all. If it were just another credal statement by which to test our own faith or the faith of others, then we haven't moved out of the old ways at all. If it were just a philosophy like "there's more in things than meets the eye," then it's just another glib tag to bandy words around. If it were an easily summarized ethic like "do to others as you'd like them to do to you," then we've heard it all before. If it were a special new kind of belief like "the humanity of Jesus and the divinity of man," then we'd just have to set up another redundant denomination. If it were just "do the Jesus thing and do your own thing," then it's just a hippie mood writ large.

And it's not just any of these things.

Of course, it includes them. It does claim, "there's more in things than meets the eye." It does insist, "do to others as you'd like them to do to you." It does believe in "the humanity of Jesus and the divinity of man." It does imply that you "do the Jesus thing and do your own thing." And it does even end up in some "credal statement" as and when necessary.

But all these are only partial definitions. Even worse, they are all attempts to put into a simple formula what is really something different from a creed, a philosophy, an ethic, a belief, or a slogan.

Let's admit it, we shall at times be forced into situations where what we are trying to point to will have to be summarized in these terms. But it won't be "the thing itself." It will be just a fumbling set of words, pointing to something which is a reality, a happening, a thing, a dynamic, an expectation, a commitment.

WHAT SHALL WE DO WITH JESUS?

The figure of Jesus has been something of an embarrassment to the churches ever since Christianity became an established "religion." Now that it is happily ceasing to be so, Christians are being forced to consider Jesus again. Now that Christendom has ended, Christians need to have good reason for being Christ-men.

Christians, by definition, are landed with Jesus, whether they like it or not. A Christianity which is mere theism, or a general pantheism, or even a non-Christ-centered panentheism, has ceased to be Christianity. So, too, has the much-vaunted "universal religion of the future" which in fact does justice to none of the world's great religious leaders.

But what is the Christ in whom the Christians are to believe? **Recent theology has tended to use the Christ figure to suit or justify widely divergent, even mutually contradictory, emphases.**

Thus, writing of the theologies of the 1960s, *The Christian Century* commented:

We have seen Jesus Christ set forth—in accelerating sequence—as a German Lutheran existentialist, a being-toward-death man, an East Harlem social worker, a disbeliever in God, a hippie, a kind of Marxist eschatologist, a Zealot. In the blur of images not a few have come to ask, "Why bother?"—not about Christ but about his volatile interpreters.[1]

Now that we are in the nineteen-seventies, even more Jesus "characters" emerge.

On the stage, we may choose between the "man of sorrows" Jesus of *Jesus Christ, Superstar*, with its rather pathetic, monotone picture of a hippie-type, mixed-up failure who, not surprisingly, confuses the all too easily supportable Judas. It is not a new pic-

[1] Editorial, *The Christian Century*, December 25, 1968, p. 1615.

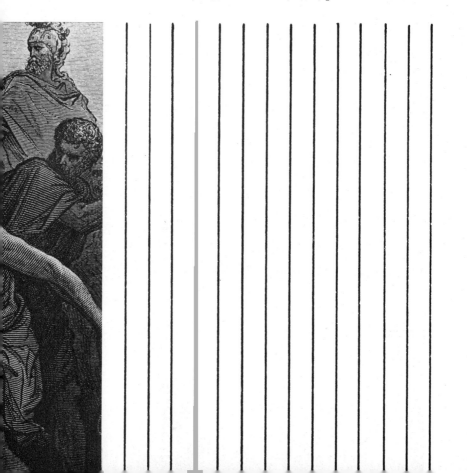

ture. Jesus Christ, the pious, good man done to death by evil be-
trayers, is a familiar figure of piety from the Middle Ages *Pietas*
to the nineteenth-century hymns. It evokes pity. Indeed, one is
even begged to believe in Jesus "because he suffered all this for
you."

Or one may choose *Godspell*. Its figure of Jesus is more to our
time's liking—Jesus the poker of fun at establishments, Jesus the
revealer of people's hidden faults and failings, Jesus the clown, the
jester, the fool, the harlequin.[2] It is a newer picture than *Superstar*. But not very much newer. And if it places Jesus firmly among
the mockers of men, it does not place him as the one in whom
everything holds together, as the New Testament claims. The
Jesus of *Godspell* evokes laughter, but not discipleship.

Yet the ethos of both *Superstar* and *Godspell* is contemporary,
urbane, usable. It evokes response, it finds points of contact. Perhaps it is futile to ask for more. No Christian "insiders" have
done better for a long time.

But it is not the whole Jesus story for our time.

What is?

Well, everyone has his own ideas. I have written a book about
Jesus, called *Secular Christ*.[3] In it, I try to show that it is as a
secular, "this-worldly" man that Jesus has most to say to us today.
But I also argue that what he has to say to us is vastly different
from what we think is the way things are. In other words, the
secular Jesus is not a modern humanistic Jesus.

If the Christians are "landed" with Jesus, they have the continuing obligation to make some sense of him. But, assuming the task
is necessary, is it *possible*? I believe that a few "red herrings" can
be dismissed for a start—as I argue in *Secular Christ*. I think that
we can know at least enough about Jesus as the Christ to make it
possible and reasonable to speak about him. **Every group has to
some extent made a Christ out of its own image, and every
Christ portrait down through history has been influenced by**

---

[2] John-Michael Tebelak, author of *Godspell*, acknowledges debt to Harvey
Cox's *Feast of Fools* (Cambridge, Mass.: Harvard University Press, 1969).

[3] John J. Vincent, *Secular Christ* (Nashville: Abingdon Press, 1968).

its social situation. But I believe there are some points at which one knows that one is definitely within or definitely outside the Jesus tradition. And, also, I believe that there are enough aspects of the Jesus figure to suit and judge every group and every age.

Thus, it is a question of the *degree* to which Jesus has been "adapted." **Some groups and ages concentrate on one aspect so much that others are ignored altogether.** In many churches to-

day, the death of Jesus for man's sins is still the hallmark of orthodoxy, even though it represents only a small (though valid) part of the total variety of New Testament attempts at interpreting Jesus. I believe that the "secular" adaptation does far more justice to the whole Jesus story. It deals with the aspects of the records about him which are most easily accessible to our understanding today. It does not attempt to dismiss the otherworldly, the magical, and the mythical aspects, but rather sees them as the framework within which Jesus and his followers lived and acted.

These are complicated matters, and the reader who wishes to pursue them must do so elsewhere. They are mentioned here solely because two of the less fortunate "results of modern scholarship" are so often taken to be "that we can know nothing about Jesus," and "that what we can know is not worth knowing because it is completely tied up in a world view which is not ours." Both these statements need now to be taken with a pinch of salt. Apart from anything else, they have not *in fact* led to people who have come through modern scholarship into ignoring Jesus. He is still around, and many who thought they had "dismissed" him are still now under his spell.

In the next few chapters, I shall put up a few pictures of Jesus which have come to have special significance among the groups of which I am writing.

Perhaps it is worth adding something else.

For twenty years, I have been a student of the New Testament, and especially the first three Gospels. Theories and interpretations come and go. They are not unimportant. There have been significant changes in emphasis. I trust there will be more. But what has most frequently been missing is some new elements in the gospel story actually "coming alive" for people today, pushing along scholarship "from the bottom." This is what I feel to be happening now, through the kind of attitudes and actions described in this book.

The Jesus people and the Jesus freaks, the Jesus revolution and the Jesus fanatics in the main represent at least a return to some of the simplicities of the gospel story. The command to all-inclusive adherence, the call to self-denial, the demand to form a new community, the joy of belonging to a chosen few—all of them, with all their good and their doubtful aspects, have reappeared. Theologically, however, the Jesus people have in the main merely repeated the theology of the old fundamentalists and evangelicals.

For many people, an intellectually honest theology is still a necessity. Let's just say that the way of the Jesus people is not our way, and that their way would not attract anyone for whom I am writing. To affirm pluralism is to affirm their right to exist. But to affirm pluralism is also to affirm *our* right to exist. And that means the right of both to see their work in the light of Jesus.

What follows is not, perhaps, so "simple" a way of understanding and living the gospel of Jesus. But it is, I believe, equally valid and equally significant. It is not so "successful" as the Jesus people, mainly because it is not so spectacular, and its people so noticeable. But it exists today as a way of looking at and living by the Gospels, in a day in which many Christians find no way of so doing.

WHAT IS IT ALL ABOUT?

The real sellout for all our careful theology is that men and women all round us are living lives of acceptance, depth, love, tenderness, significance, value, meaning, passion, forgiveness, atonement, self-sacrifice—*without us!* And we, the theologians, are supposed to be the keepers of the secrets of life and death! And all they hear from us is insensitive cantations, clever concepts, more words. If we use the word "God" to describe the cantations, the concepts, the words, then of course "God" is dead, and everyman today must be an atheist. The word "God" is dead to us not because it represents no reality, but because men living in reality cannot see anything in reality to which it points.

But there is another possibility. Perhaps the Christian church has been made the steward of the inner mysteries and secrets of ordinary secular human existence, which are only discernible now in an age when the "religious dimension" has all but disappeared. Indeed, I believe that the things about Jesus are really the inner core and reality and significance already present within the life of every man, woman, and child. The *incarnation* of Jesus is basically *about* every human being's attainment of dignity and acceptance through submission and subjection to the demands of the secular, physical, bodily world which is ours. **The ministry of Jesus is basically about everyman's obligation to serve and minister.** The *parables* are basically *about* the hidden significance of

what everyman is doing all the time, in every place, in every land. The *acceptance of sinners* by Jesus is basically *about* how everyman judges himself by his attitude to others. *The disciples* are basically *about* the necessity for oddballs and square-pegs as well as technocrats if man's existence is to be whole. The *death* of Jesus is basically *about* how everyman, whether Christian or not, touches significance through death to himself. **The resurrection of Jesus is basically about the constant emergence of new life through the willing death of the past.**

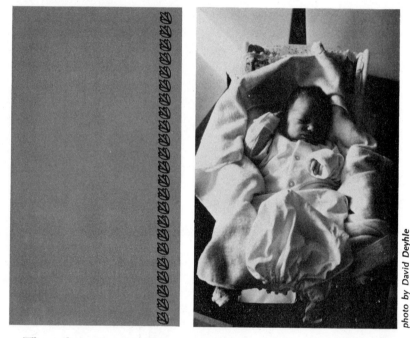

photo by David Deyhle

Thus, the mysteries of Jesus are not pieces of truth about a few people called Christians who "opt into them" at baptism, crisis, and death, or even at worship or at communion. Rather, they are the whole truth of what is happening to everybody all the time, in vocation, marriage and family relationships, politics and leisure —the whole life of man.

This is, I believe, the authentic Christian radicalism for our time.

It is about "human existence at its most human." But it is *simultaneously* about Christ experience at its most christocentric. It is that Jesus represents "the way things are for all men." Thus, Joseph W. Mathews:

This eschatological hero is then the portraiture of what human living actually is. He is an unqualified delineation of the human style of life. He is a model of faith-filled living. A model is a design of the way things are. It is a construct of the manner in which things are understood to function. In dealing with subjects rather than objects, as in the case at hand, where the model is a personage, perhaps the "exemplar" would be a more fitting term. The Christ hero is a model or exemplar of what is going on where unmitigated human living is taking place.[1]

So if, in answer to the Christian claim that "all the mysteries of life and death are hid in Christ," modern man presses the question "what mysteries?" this theology is not without answers.

Of the mystery of God there is little, but enough, to be said. Jesus felt that his "heavenly parent" was indiscriminate in his provisions through nature, demanding in his requirements of those who wished to be his "children," and a judge who rewarded or forgave as he pleased. Jesus appropriated part only of these—the stringent requirements and the arbitrary forgiveness. The indiscriminate regard in nature and the ultimate judgment remain hidden.

The secular Jesus does not come to "reveal God"—he comes to reveal the world in which he claims God has hidden himself. We cannot say that Jesus' main teaching is that there is a "personal, loving, heavenly Father." That is only part of it. And the figure of "father" is only one among several that Jesus, like his contemporaries, used of God. Its theological significance, particularly in the sense of a "personal" God, should not be overstretched.

But there are the *deeds*, and they reveal the mysteries of *life*. And to be a Christian is to make this leap of faith that the *life* of

[1] Joseph W. Mathews, *The Eschatological Hero* (Chicago: Ecumenical Institutes, 1969).

photo by Ronald Benedict

Christ is not ultimately to be mocked or set at naught within the humanity which is his. **Thus, my problem is not how to relate the churches' Christ to a world without him, but how to relate a world which shouts Christ at me to a church without him.**

So, then, let us summarize our attempt as a threefold effort.

1. The christological core of faith is *something unique and radical about the secular, about this world. Hence, a "secular Christ."*

2. This part of the christological core of faith is *especially relevant to our modern secular world. Hence a "Christ for today."*

3. This secular Christ is vital to a new understanding of *the church and Christian discipleship. Hence, a "radical Christ."*

THE JESUS THING

LET'S PLAY A GAME

I set a riddle to the rulers of the land:
Is your God's law dearer than a man's right hand?
Would you be sons of God or sons of man?
And don't you hear the children for they understand?

    Let's Play a Game:
    Let's pretend their ox or ass has fallen lame,
    And let's see if God's law remains the same.

I set a riddle as I hung on a tree
As I stretched out my arms across eternity
As I drew the whole world in from the ends of the sea
And I gave it to the children who were following me.

    Let's Play a Game:
    Let's pretend that love is each man's name
    Let's see if the world remains the same.

Here's a riddle of the fire that is the strength of the weak,
The wealth of the poor and the power of the meek,
That the blind can see; of which the dumb can speak,
And a fire only found in the children who will seek.

    Let's Play a Game:
    You're the ring of roses, I'm the flame.
    Just to bring this fire was why I came.

Michael Stewart, *More Songs*
from Notting Hill

WHO YOU ARE IS WHERE YOU ARE

Then Jesus went to Nazareth, where he had been brought up, and on the Sabbath day he went as usual to the synagogue. He stood up to read the Scriptures, and was handed the book of the prophet Isaiah. He unrolled the scroll and found the place where it is written:
"The Spirit of the Lord is upon me.
He has anointed me to preach the Good News to the poor,
He has sent me to proclaim liberty to the captives,
And recovery of sight to the blind,
To set free the oppressed,
To announce the year when the Lord will save his people!"
Jesus rolled up the scroll, gave it back to the attendant, and sat down. All the people in the synagogue had their eyes fixed on him. He began speaking to them: "This passage of scripture has come true today, as you heard it being read."

Luke 4:16-21 TEV

Who you are is where you are.
You cannot "pretend" easily if your backyard is on their street. And you can only be "one" with them if you are with them.
Today, we find it impossible to talk about what a person is "in essence," as if it were different from what he is "in action." The way a man appears is the way he is. And the way a man appears is ultimately linked with where he is, in history, in society, in culture.
Thus, the basic theology of Jesus is an attempt to say that God is where Jesus is, and that Jesus is what he is doing in the place where he stands alongside men. Let us see what this basic insight might mean in terms of the contemporary "Jesus thing."

Jesus: A Christology of Action. The calling of Jesus as man achieves and indicates the secularization of the holy, the realization of the ideal of the righteous, the localization of the universal, the temporalization of the eternal. Now, only the secularization, the realization, the localization, and the temporalization in Jesus are to be heeded. This is the gospel of "incarnation" which cuts off all other roads to the holy, righteous, universal, and eternal, in order to open them anew for all in Jesus.

Thus, we derive the clue of *incarnation,* "Inmundation."

Negatively, this is the word for man's long search after meaning, faith, religion, philosophy, idealism, ideology. Each must be rejected insofar as it attempts to go beyond the secular, human situation, in order to bring in some world view which begins outside and then makes the secular and human subservient to itself. The business of theology is not any form of scholarly, departmental, or intellectual gamesmanship. **The theologian as a Christian theologian only becomes what he is when he stops playing conceptual games, and allows the Christ mysteries to confront him within secular history and secular man.**

photo by Ronald Benedict

Positively, this opens for the disciple of Jesus an enormous and boundless optimism concerning the human situation; *a new humanism.* But because of the incarnation it must be a *christocentric humanism,* or, better, a *christocentric humanness.* The disciple's concern is not just man's natural existence today, but rather a new style of life and existence based on the real presence of Christ in the world.

Practically, this implies a complete openness on the part of the disciple toward all men, and therefore to all politics, convictions, influences, reforms, and movements among men. The Christian is thus a "pragmatist" rather than a man of principle, as a basic stance, because he ventures to assume a hidden dynamic in existence and history which it was the purpose of the incarnation to initiate—a veritable "God-with-man-ness"—which demands, not simply that he heeds and applauds man as such (that is to say very little), but that he heeds the Jesus man to see what humanity could be and, already at its best or possibly most unselfconscious, tries to be.

The style of the church as the liberated group thus oscillates between a complete acceptance of man as he is, on the one hand, and an assertion of a radically different kind of Jesus humanity, on the other hand. Humanist radicals among Christians over the past decade or two have emphasized the former. And it has been important to stress, against the background of so many centuries of oppression and dehumanization at the hands of churches and church dogmas and disciplines, that the Christian is first and foremost a human being, a man among other men, a man who lives, eats, loves, and creates community and significance in exactly the same way as every other man does. Yet it is now important to begin to stress also the other side of the matter. Christians are not merely men, they are Jesus-men. Jesus is not merely a man, he is God's man, the anointed man. A new Christian radicalism is now emerging, which takes seriously not just the humanist strain, but also the radically different kind of humanism and humanity presented and represented in Jesus.

The place or the group that seeks to embody and represent this dynamic of "the liberated life" and "the Jesus life as liberation" at one and the same time stands in danger from both anonymous humanists (who do not name the name) and also unseeing Christians (who name the name but do not see the humanity). But precisely this task is the knife-edge and the thrill, the impossibility and the possibility, of being a Jesus follower now.

WHERE THE ACTION IS

John's disciples told him about all these things. John called two of them to him and sent them to the Lord to ask him, "Are you the one John said was going to come, or should we expect someone else?" When they came to Jesus they said, "John the Baptist sent us to ask, 'Are you the one he said was going to come, or should we expect someone else?'" At that very time Jesus healed many people from their sicknesses, diseases, and evil spirits, and gave sight to many blind people.

He answered John's messengers: "Go back and tell John what you have seen and heard: the blind can see, the lame can walk, the lepers are made clean, the deaf can hear, the dead are raised to life, and the Good News is preached to the poor. How happy is he who has no doubts about me!"

Luke 7:18-23 TEV

John the Baptist had been a successful revivalist preacher until Jesus came along. Then John gave it all up, hoping Jesus was "the coming one" whom he had announced. John was jailed, and the reports of Jesus' works of healing reached him. But healing is not messiahship! Had Jesus deceived John? Hence the frantic, agonized question, "Are you the one John said was going to come, or should we expect someone else?"

The reply of Jesus is beautiful or impertinent, according to taste. He just goes on "doing his thing." And even when he does get around to sending back a message, it is only "go back and tell John what you have seen and heard." Jesus cannot be separated from his action. You must see the action, and let it judge you—and happy the man who, though it be arbitrary, earthy, and unspectacular, is not offended at it. Where the action is, there is "grace and all blessedness."

What does this lead to today?

Ministry: The Healing of the Kingdon. **The healings and exorcisms of Jesus achieve and indicate that God is not a God of providence, but ranges himself positively in Jesus against all that robs man of wholeness, and actively works for man's total well-being.** This is the gospel of "salvation" insofar that it brings relief to those who never "believe" but merely allow that miracle of healing to happen.

Here, our clue is surely *liberation*.

Negatively, this means the rejection of *religious* attempts to secure wholeness. To all schemes of individuals to "save their life" comes the call of Jesus to "lose life for my sake, and the Good News' sake." To all religious attempts to "get right with God" Jesus says that man must "preach, teach, heal, and cast out devils." To all Western versions and perversions of Christendom, exorcism does not mean adding human sophistications or compensations to the affluent life, but costly global service and sacrifice. It demands that there be no part-time Christians, no Christians who avail themselves of the best the world can give, and add to it spiritual blessings—"All this and Heaven too!"

Positively, this opens up for all men in Jesus a new *vocation*. It demands that healing be the call of all. It demands that the little company of these "disciples to the Kingdom" shall be alongside those who minister.

In practical and more immediate terms, it means that those faithful to Jesus will be the place where a new understanding of economics is manifest. The disciple is the healer, the steward of creation, the "daysman" in industry, the experimental farmer in the African bush, the pioneer in human sciences, the outrider in community action, the "new radical" for politics. He is the man who can be heard by the economists, the futurologists, the politicians, the sociologists, for he speaks from the irrefutable personal commitment of his own vocation and experience.

Yet, of course, here as everywhere, the disciple must ensure that he makes clear that he is merely holding overt and clear witness to a truth which is for all men. In this case, the truth is, "the greatest man is the man who is the servant of all." The life of Jesus has made plain that the question of vocation is not a matter of working out inner potentialities so much as responding to the neighbor who evokes the disciple's concern. Equally, it has made clear that messiahship for Jesus, and thus acceptability for the disciple, depends upon "doing the will of the Father," that is, upon love of the neighbor. Furthermore, it has made plain that discipleship to Jesus consists in doing the deeds of Jesus, not in calling him "Lord, Lord." When the disciples seek to restrict the use of the Jesus name to those who openly follow him, Jesus tells them that "he who is not against us is for us." When, on the other hand, the disciple seeks to take for granted his position of discipleship, Jesus warns that "he who is not with me is against me."

The deeds of discipleship are done in the modern world wherever technology, medicine, agriculture, and every branch of science and art perform their true function in building structures and agencies for man's wholeness. This is the way in which all men *may* be part of the Kingdom's good works. But, equally, the conscious and intentional disciple of Jesus is not allowed to take refuge in this rather vague and nebulous kind of "vocation"—which, in the inscrutable rationalization of man, can only too easily cover every imaginable activity (and for others, perhaps does!). The conscious and intentional disciple seeks the place and the work which crucially need to be done, which impinge most upon his conscience, which are the places most ignored by others, and most like to Jesus' work among the forgotten, the outcast, the rejected, the disadvantaged, the incurably sick, the alien.

THERE'S MORE IN LIFE

Now, to what can I compare the people of this day? What are they like? They are like children sitting in the market place. One group shouts to the other, "We played wedding music for you, but you would not dance! We sang funeral songs, but you would not cry!" John the Baptist came, and he fasted and drank no wine, and you said, "He is a madman!" The Son of Man came, and he ate and drank, and you said, "Look at this man! He is a glutton and wine-drinker, and is a friend of tax collectors and outcasts!" God's wisdom, however, is shown to be true by all who accept it.

Luke 7:31-35 TEV

Whatever you do, not only will you not please everybody—you will offend somebody!

And the purpose of the parable is to show that the true significance of what people do is almost invariably hidden from them. A man mourns—and all the people do is demand laughter. A man eats and drinks with outsiders—and all the people do is demand asceticism.

But what was *really* happening in John? And what is *really* happening in Jesus? The parables rarely "explain" it all. Rather, they suggest that there's always more in things than meets the eye, that there's always more in life than one thought of at first.

"The Kindgom" is the name that Jesus gives to this "thing" in life which is "the more," "the hidden"—in New Testament terms, "the messianic," the "accepted by God," the "sign of God's rule."

The "Jesus thing" seeks to take account of it also.

Parables: The Hiddenness of the Kingdom. The preachings and parables of Jesus achieve and indicate the utter secularization of God and the Kingdom of God, and proclaim that a Kingdom is now *hidden* within apparently purely secular, selfish, political, or mercenary actions. The gospel of Jesus is that men deal with God through the secular, the selfish, the political, the mercenary; and that they do not deal with him or the Kingdom *directly,* but only through these things.

Here our clue is the *Kingdom.*

Negatively, the Kingdom closes all religious attempts to get to God. Moreover, the Kingdom must not be understood as something existing only in a spiritual sense (old liberals and old neo-orthodox), or something which is simply seen as "Christendom's contribution to history." Thus, we would hesitate on contemporary definition of the Kingdom as "humanization" (van Leeuwen), or even "making human life totally human" (Paul Lehmann), or the "growth of love" in a continuous evolutionary sense (Teilhard de Chardin). Likewise, the Kingdom is not something achievable in history (Social Gospel and Marxism), or something represented to us by our contemporary society (Harvey Cox), or something which is a future historical reality imposing itself into the present (Jürgen Moltmann).[1] The Kingdom is thus the *end* of all historical or apologetic or culture-determined views of man's history. It releases him from any historical "destiny."

Positively, the Kingdom is the latent *dynamic within* the human spirit, the continuing evolution of the universe, the contemporary humanism, the process of history, man's contemporary society, and the historical terminus. It affirms each of these by being not an added "element" to them, but by being the dimension at which they become, within the limitations of themselves, part of the recurring emergent significance which is neither ontological nor evolutionary but dynamic. This opens up for the Christian a dual

[1] The authors cited would provide a good introduction to the contemporary theological debate, in the context of which the gross summary is written. They are: A. Th. van Leeuwen, *Christianity in World History* (New York: Charles Scribner's Sons, 1966); Paul L. Lehmann, *Ethics in a Christian Context* (New York: Harper & Row, 1963); Teilhard de Chardin, *The Phenomenon of Man* (New York: Harper & Brothers, 1965); Harvey Cox, *The Secular City* (New York: Macmillan Paperbacks, 1965); Jürgen Moltmann, *Theology of Hope* (New York: Harper & Row, 1967). For a discussion of some of these issues, cf. my *Secular Christ,* esp. pp. 219-28.

privilege and a task. On the one hand, he has a *ministry of identifi-cation*: of seeing the places where events, movements, tendencies, persons, or groups seem to reflect the possibilities of healing. On the other hand, he operates under the hesitation necessitated by the good news of *the Kingdom's hiddenness*. And this is good news: because it means that man is delivered from ultimate pre-sumption, from pride and overconfidence. He must act, and act boldly; but he still does it "in faith"—as if there were always "more than meets the eye" in it all.

In practice, the doctrine, like truth, is not always easy to follow. The disciple oscillates between awaiting, recognizing, and hailing the signs, yet realizing that he cannot recognize the hidden King-dom. He describes the lineaments and knows they are at work, but he does not say "lo here" or "lo there." The disciple therefore operates not simply with "the world as the agenda" but with a hidden agenda also—an agenda of secret understanding, expecta-tion, and intention. But—the disciple is also not so naïve as to miss what seems to him the present evidences and indications. The ministry of identification means the seeking out of the poor, the disinherited, the victims, the handicapped, the disadvantaged. The disciple's human strength or resources are used for them, and by his identification with them he may proclaim, so far as he can see, the hidden Kingdom's coming near to them and to him in their actual situation.

LET'S PLAY A GAME

Then he turned to the woman and said to Simon: "Do you see this woman? I came into your home, and you gave me no water for my feet, but she has washed my feet with her tears and dried them with her hair. You did not welcome me with a kiss, but she has not stopped kissing my feet since I came. You provided no oil for my head, but she has covered my feet with perfume. I tell you, then, the great love she has shown proves that her many sins have been forgiven. Whoever has been forgiven little, however, shows only a little love." Then Jesus said to the woman, "Your sins are forgiven." The others sitting at the table began to say to themselves, "Who is this, who even forgives sins?" But Jesus said to the woman, "Your faith has saved you; go in peace."

Luke 7:44-50 TEV

How can "the great love she has shown" prove that "her many sins have been forgiven"? Does she show the love because her sins are forgiven? Or is the love she is showing the means whereby the sins are forgiven? Perhaps the second. For what "saved" her was her "faith," that is, her bold and presumptuous action.

If the purpose of Jesus was to get people somehow or other into the thing which was for their ultimate good (the Kingdom, love of God, discipleship, forgiveness, peace), then his method was to put himself in the way of actions whereby those people could avail themselves of it. He has to be prepared for his feet to be washed. He has to let the game be played which is forgiveness.

And the footwashing is not so much "an outward and visible sign" of the inward grace of forgiveness; rather, it is the *means* whereby the forgiveness "works," and is accepted by the parties concerned. It is an "acted parable" of one person being freed from sins, and another person freeing sins from the first.

Such action parables are part of the "Jesus thing."

Acted Parables: The Forgiveness of the Kingdom. The meals of Jesus with outcasts and prostitutes achieve and indicate the forgiveness of God present in the deeds of Jesus, which *is* forgiveness in "acted parable," and is seen as such by the scribes and Pharisees. The gospel is that all men now stand before the feast of God's presence. God eats now in Jesus with all men, who love or hate him, accept or reject him, hidden in the person of their neighbor.

photo by Ronald Benedict

God now in Jesus forgives all men inasmuch as and precisely when they have forgiven their neighbor. God's forgiveness can be taken for granted: man's forgiveness of man is all that is required to avail oneself of it.

Here, our clue is *imagination*.

Negatively, forgiveness ceases to be a religious operation. It is not the way whereby a great barrier is overcome between a holy, separate God and wayward man. Rather, forgiveness, being utterly between men, is the dynamic whereby obstacles to wholeness, reconciliation, and joy are removed. How are they removed? Not by bringing in a "third party" called "God," but by imaginatively and redemptively shifting the basis of equality and acceptance over into the other person's situation.

Positively, this means giving ourselves to *acted parables*. Forgiveness is the technique by which, in self-identification with my neighbor, I allow him to be other than himself, and expect him to be more than I am. Forgiveness is the technique by which I understand that I must above all be *vulnerable*, so that my neighbor also can be reconciled by forgiving me. But since both my forgiveness and his can be mediated only by deed rather than word, I must seek and allow him to seek acted parables whereby forgiveness can be embodied, dramatized and extended.

Thus, the contemporary forms of the meals with publicans and sinners are "happenings" which inform them of the new situation open before them. In specific situations, these might even become embodied in institutions—the open youth center, the cross-cultural club, the interracial community, the open door to Communists, the global consciousness and witness. Only so can the disciples of Jesus "bring the nations in," without converting them, but not without changing them. Reconciliation occurs only where there is forgiveness, and forgiveness is the limit of fellow-feeling and imagination, and imagination needs to be clothed in acted parables for all to see, in which they may even find themselves being forgiven and reconciled.

In the Gospels, the disciples become involved in the work of Jesus in acted parables. Jesus indicates the acceptance of all men, their sharing in the messianic banquet, and the disciples' place as servants within it, in the feedings of the five thousand. The actions of Jesus *are* "God coming near," and the actions already carry the significance of the reality standing behind them. In fact, man does not now deal directly with the reality standing behind them (God,

or the Kingdom of God), but deals only with Jesus, and deals only
with Jesus in the form of the controversial and problematic actions
which embody what he is and says, and which give every person
the chance to become also involved in it. So the disciples also must
"act their part," the Jesus part, for in response to them, people
respond to Jesus, and in responding to Jesus, they respond to God.
Thus the disciples' entering a city *is* "God coming near," and if
people do not see it, the dust can be shaken off the disciples' feet
"as a testimony against them," because they did not see the true
significance of the artless incidents of Kingdom-disciples bidding
peace upon a house.

And if only the world—and the disciples—would be content
thus to be "tricked" into being released, through this technique of
acting as if things were different, then the dynamic of mutual reconciliation would also be let loose. Without it, there is only
straightforwardness, and decency, and honesty, and self-satisfaction
—and thus pride, insensitivity, and standing on dignity.

JESUS PEOPLE

At that same time Jesus was filled with joy by the Holy Spirit,
and said: "O Father, Lord of heaven and earth! I thank you because
you have shown to the unlearned what you have hidden from the wise
and learned. Yes, Father, this was done by your own choice and
pleasure.

"My Father has given me all things: no one knows who the Son
is except the Father, and no one knows who the Father is except the
Son and those to whom the Son wants to reveal him."

Then Jesus turned to the disciples and said to them privately:
"How happy are you, to see the things you see! For many prophets
and kings, I tell you, wanted to see what you see, but they could not,
and to hear what you hear, but they did not."

Luke 10:21-24 TEV

The disciples in the gospel story are the people who are "inside"
the Jesus movement. They are the "Jesus people."

Often—not to say invariably—they are in the wrong. Being privy to the secret does not in fact make them very wise. Especially in Mark, they appear as the comic relief, or the chorus line, or the buffoons: at best, they are the "supporting cast" who show up the star by their following him, but hardly add to the story except by their mistakes.[1]

Luke softens this rather—and in the passage above records this little thanksgiving for them. Regardless of their incompetence, they are "inside." They are with the boss, the chairman, the master. And, when it comes to the push, they will stand by him—at least as far as Gethsemane.

It's part of the "Jesus thing" that there have to be disciples.

Discipleship: The Faith That Works. The call to discipleship which Jesus addresses to some achieves and indicates the possibility of man's conscious and intentional involvement in and identification with the mysteries of Jesus, which in fact apply to all, but which are openly avowed only by the few. The gospel is that man can be a fellow worker through Jesus with God, if he will take up the cross and follow the way God's grace provides. The gospel is that a man is "justified by trusting" (faith), that is, setting off his whole life as an act which is ludicrous and unfulfilling unless the Jesus-God is behind it.

The clue here is the *secret discipline.*

Negatively, this means the end of old Israel or new church in the static sense. Only when the ministry of Jesus in the world is seen and demanded does there arise a church. The church is thus not constituted by those who "believe the gospel" but by those who "act the good news," that is, embody those saving ministries which they have seen in Jesus. The church does not exist where "the gospel is faithfully proclaimed and the sacraments duly administered," but where the Jesus-centered life of being called and being sent out to preach, teach, heal, and cast out devils is continued.

---

[1] Cf. my critical study of discipleship in Mark, entitled *Disciple and Lord* (forthcoming).

Positively, this means a community of people who are prepared
to operate upon the assumption that the dynamic of the Kingdom
is present in the world and available forever as a way to imitate.
It means that the disciple does not think that he uniquely operates
the ministries which are for the wholeness of the world, but that
he consciously and intentionally sets himself under them. He
takes the commands, "teach, preach, heal, and cast out devils,"
"take up your cross and follow," and "lose your life for my sake
and the good news' sake" as a new life-style of freedom for others
through being with and in Jesus. He thus comes together with
other Jesus followers to repeat the words and deeds of Jesus and
the words and deeds of secular significance, simultaneously—
which is Christian worship.

Practically, this means, I am afraid, a vocation of the disciple to
be not only a sign to the world but also a sign to the church by
being the *radical church,* or even better, the *para-church.* So far as
the institutional and established churches are concerned, it means
that all spiritual escapisms, ecumenical rationalizations, clerical re-
groupings, theological enterprises and congregational barbecues
stand under the judgment, "What Do Ye More Than the World?"
So far as the would-be disciple is concerned it means that all
renewal groups, underground churches, radical churches, non-
churches, para-churches, creative disaffiliations, new churches, and
middle-class house churches stand under a similar word, "What
do ye more than the first lot?" Everywhere, we need front-room
churches, restaurant churches, store-front churches, ecumenical
parties, frontier ministries, groups, mission agencies, community
houses, and whatever else the ingenuity of small groups can get
going. And they must be the church anew, not for themselves,
but as prophetic signs for the rest. Everywhere we need signs of
men "leaving their nets," not in order to escape from the burden
of tiresome pagans in the church, but in order to be his witnesses
even to them, as they carry out ministry in the world. For precisely
in the old church, men are desperate for signs of action, for gospel
action is the lifeblood of the whole church.

Only when we have people perched on the edge of existence

will we know why Dietrich Bonhoeffer called for a "secret discipline" (arcane discipline). And only when we need it, and feel that we need it, will we know whether we wanted all the renewal things about worship, prayer, devotion, and "community." But then, we will probably find that all of them come to us again in even more different forms, because they are the result of the Jesus commitment, and not yet another attempt to precipitate it devotionally, or provide a buffer for it.

LORD OF THE DANCE

"I came to set the earth on fire, and how I wish it were already kindled! I have a baptism to receive, and how distressed I am until it is over! Do you suppose that I came to bring peace to the world? Not peace, I tell you, but division. From now on a family of five will be divided, three against two, two against three. Fathers will be against their sons, and sons against their fathers; mothers will be against their daughters, and daughters against their mothers; mothers-in-law will be against their daughters-in-law, and daughters-in-law against their mothers-in-law."

Luke 12:49-53 TEV

Two things are very clear about self-sacrifice in the Gospels.

First, it "has to be." Long before the cross, the disciples are told to be cross-carriers, people on the long, ignominious procession to death, people laughed at and mocked, people condemned to die as political guerillas. And this "crucifixion dance," open to the world, they are to take up "daily."

Secondly, it is done "for others." Suffering is vicarious. Self-sacrifice is for the fullness of life which others can come to in the wake of it.

So it is not peace, but division. What father wants to see his son, on whom he has lavished education and money, taking to the road and living the life of a penniless preacher? What mother wants to see her daughter, on whom she has showered affection and pride, leaving the university to work unpaid among down-and-outs? What mother-in-law wants to see her daughter-in-law, for whose offspring she has such great hopes, settling in the inner city? So it is not peace, but division. For other people's sake, for the world's sake, for Christ's sake. It's just part of "the thing."

Self-sacrifice: The Gift of Significance. The sufferings and cross of Jesus achieve and indicate God's being at the mercy of his creatures. The gospel is that God repudiates justice and power, and uses self-sacrifice to open up a new and living way whereby others may bring redemption through self-offering, that is, through Christ.

Here, the clue is self-sacrifice.

Negatively, this is a judgment on the church's invariable "preaching of the cross." Vicariousness does not mean that because Jesus has gone to death, we do not need to go, but rather that, now he has gone to death, we are free and able to do so. The crucifixion is not, therefore, something the church "glories in," except insofar as it is prepared (with Paul) to have it's own sufferings and allow them also to be "glory." **Jesus has initiated a fellowship of fellow workers, dying and rising with him, not a mass of worshipers clinging to "the benefits of his passion."**

photo by Richard Lee

Positively, this means that the disciple understands the mystery of vicariousness as *unilateral initiative*. He knows that the world can only be won to its own redemption as he has been won to his. That is, it can only be won by a "trick"—by the disciple himself being so worldly that the world mistakes him for itself, and finds itself following his way of humanness, vocation, identification with the needy, acted parables, and secret discipline for others, and thus, willy-nilly, encountering the living techniques which are its own salvation. All the disciple has to do is to be content to be the unilateral initiator, the vicarious savior, the experimental guinea pig, the "Christ who perishes in every age for those who have no imagination" (Bernard Shaw).

Specific initiatives naturally follow. Christians are "the Saviors of God." They believe that life follows death. Therefore, their task in the situation of world poverty is to demonstrate their faith in the possibility of salvation for all by the vicarious self-giving of the few; only then will the church have any ground for appealing to the politicians on the basis of "justice for all." The Christians must discover how to "give their life a ransom for many" in the hard currency of specific acts of self-sacrificial generosity, not simply because "reparations" are in order, but because world justice hangs not on equalization but on some people in some places toppling the military-industrial complex by a radical death which will speak. The Christians in nation churches likewise must find a way to *be* the new internationalism so that, by their own death, a new world community may live—and by that small life, a *theatron* of the whole universal brotherhood at last appear. (A *theatron* is a spectacle, a performance, a show, a piece of theater. It is the word used by Paul of his own suffering in I Cor. 4:9, by which he has been made into "an open show" for all to see. Vicariousness and unilateral initiative are both represented in the *theatron* idea, as implied here.)

The church thus carries its witness in deeds to the truth that operates everywhere and in everything—that significance, or eternal life, or the Kingdom of God, or value, or acceptance belongs to a technique of identification, self-sacrifice, and vicarious suffering.

Where these things are faithfully and costingly persevered with, there is indeed a foretaste of "heaven," because there is a genuine fellowship with the sufferings of Christ. And this is an utterly secular mystery—a presence of whatever can be called "ultimate" or "transcendent" already in the midst of the most unlikely human or political action. For that human or political action is the means whereby wholeness, salvation, healing are brought to the needy.

KEEP RISING FROM THE DEAD

An argument came up among the disciples as to which of them should be thought of as the greatest. Jesus said to them: "The kings of this world have power over their people, and the rulers are called 'Friends of the People.' But this is not the way it is with you; rather, the greatest one among you must be like the youngest, and the leader must be like the servant. Who is greater, the one who sits down to eat or the one who serves him? The one who sits down, of course. But I am among you as one who serves.

"You have stayed with me all through my trials; and just as my Father has given me the right to rule, so I will make the same agreement with you. You will eat and drink at my table in my Kingdom, and you will sit on thrones to judge the twelve tribes of Israel."

Luke 22:24-30 TEV

The long arguments about resurrection in the New Testament have tended to obscure the simple reason behind the resurrection motif. It is: that Jesus is alive; that the Jesus thing is unconquerable; that despite the evidence there is an ultimate future only for him and his way.

So, resurrection is the truth that the one who serves is the one who reigns, the one who dies is the one who lives, the one who washes the pots is the one who sits at the feast, the one perpetually judged or misjudged by others is the one who ultimately is the judge of all. Not because he is better, or good, or righteous, or humble, or generous, but because he has been caught in the Jesus thing, which finally holds the world together, and holds all men together, which is for him righteousness, joy, and peace. So he "keeps rising from the dead," as George MacDonald's hymn, "O Lord of life," says. The resurrection of Jesus is manifest in his secular existence: the "Jesus thing" has him again.

Resurrection: Jesus Our Contemporary. The resurrection renders contemporary the whole pattern of redemption in Jesus. The resurrection of Jesus is the ultimate imprimatur upon Jesus, the final acceptance and ratification by God of the whole ministry whereby the world is brought to its redemption. It is the "sign" of the Jesus deeds as true and valid for all time. The gospel is that this whole way of Jesus is forever accepted and significant before God, and thus the privilege and obligation of man to live by. It is the good news that heaven and earth were meant for Jesus, and that heaven and earth work the Jesus way.

Here, the clue is *acceptance*.

Negatively, the resurrection has to be rescued from personal salvation piety. It is not the assurance of "eternal life" to all and sundry. It is not a Christian super-plus on the top of affluence now. Christianity is not "all this and heaven too."

Positively, the resurrection is the "yes" of God to mankind. It is the "yes" of God to the life of incarnation, healing, identification, forgiveness, discipleship, and crucifixion. It is *the promise* that the man, family, community, nation, generation, or even church that loses life will find it. It is the promise of hope—the promise of acceptance. It comes to those who do not look for it, but who believe that what they are about are the Jesus mysteries of existence.

What does it mean in practice? Perhaps all that can be said is that, occasionally, erratically, here in this world, it means for the disciple *the promise*—the promise of significance occasionally breaking through, the promise of the Kingdom, the dawn occasionally of a new day, the appearance occasionally of success and even human acceptance. Perhaps it is best of all to be regarded as "joy," as *hilaritas*, as the unlooked-for sense of the presence of the One in whom all things hold together in the midst of the battle.

In secular terms, "resurrection" happens whenever there is success in reconciling opposers, or wealth where there had been poverty, or justice where there had been oppression. Yet resurrection is never a constant state. It is always the condition which brings momentary or at least temporary fulfillment in the aftermath of the way of involvement, healing, identification, forgiveness, discipline, and self-sacrifice. Resurrection occurs only in the place where there has been crucifixion. But in every other place, the whole mystery of secular redemption has to be started all over again—the Jesus people or the Jesus actions must always begin at incarnation, never at resurrection. And the man or the situation that has been "raised to newness of life" knows that in many more parts of life he must go back to the beginning again. Thus, the Christian is committed not to revolution but to continuing revolution. Thus, the Christian is committed to wholehearted involvement in specific acts and policies, but when he has seen them brought to fruition, he does not imagine that anything permanent has been obtained, but only one section of existence rectified temporarily for the salvation of men.

Therefore, the church also can only live "in the spirit of the resurrection" by living the whole Jesus mystery through again and again. And if, in its worship, or hymnody, or devotion, it occasionally seems to act as if it already enjoyed the resurrection existence, it must find means precisely in its worship, hymns, and devotion to indicate that it is the whole Christ pattern that it lives by and bodies forth, and not simply a perpetual blessedness of Easter joy. Yet also, and with equal force, it must have the impertinence to rejoice, to dance, to shout, and to dramatize its moments of fulfillment as what indeed they are—the resurrection of Jesus from the grave.

HOLDING ALL THINGS TOGETHER

Christ is the visible likeness of the invisible God. He is the first-born Son, superior to all created things. For by him God created everything in heaven and on earth, the seen and the unseen things, including spiritual powers, lords, rulers, and authorities. God created the whole universe through him and for him. He existed before all things, and in union with him all things have their proper place.

Colossians 1:15-17 TEV

In union with Christ, "all things have their proper place," says the Today's Version. The New English Bible is nearer to the Greek when it translates: "all things are held together in him." The Jerusalem Bible has: "he holds all things in unity."

Parousia: Jesus the Ultimate. Christianity is the claim that "the things of Jesus" are the only ultimate things; that everything is "held together" by them; that whatever God there is, is a God who supports them; that whatever truth there is, is truth "as it is in Jesus"; that whatever values or techniques or methods or operations within secular history which work for the wholeness of life are the "working" of the Jesus thing.[1] All the New Testament passages (a complex and mutually contradictory maze) referring to judgment, future resurrection, agelong life, the parousia, the new coming, the coming Kingdom, etc. have this fundamental concern: to show in whatever mythology can be laid hands upon, that Jesus is the definitive and universal fact, now at work in the world, and finally to be made clear (in whatever form!) as the only thing that was really going on that mattered at all.

This simple Jesus-centered view does not lead to exclusivism or superiority. Rather, it leads to humble willingness to be in on the "act." The "action church" or the "liberated church" knows itself to be in the vanguard of a theological reformation greater than that of the sixteenth century. For Luther and the medievalists, faith was that whereby a man was saved, and the debate was only about *right* faith. For the radical, faith does not consist in "belief" or "understanding" or even "commitment" understood in a general sense; and, of course, it does not consist in "works" in the faith/

[1] For the New Testament statements on parousia as ultimacy, see my *Secular Christ,* pp. 154-59.

works debate sense. *Faith consists in the willingness to work as if the Jesus thing was working.*

That is, faith is action based on the presupposition that the Jesus action is significant and operative and ultimately the only thing working on earth. Thus, the radical *acts*, and thus indicates

KIERKEGAARDIAN PIG DEMONSTRATING A LEAP OF FAITH

From A Porcine History of Philosophy and Religion by James Taylor. © 1972 by Abingdon Press.

that he "has faith." He acts "in faith," but equally his faith is "in" his acts. For his acts are the only possible way in which he can say "yes, I believe the Jesus thing is going on and, in the end, despite its hiddenness, naïvety, unsuccess, and vulnerability, is the *only* thing that is going on."

Only when the primacy of action, dynamics, living itself has been asserted, can or should there be a return to the passive aspect of Christianity which has been so determinative for devotion and worship for so long. The whole of morning and evening prayer is based on the psalms, whose main message is: "Stand by me, God. The world has a down on me." The church has glorified suffering in a subjective sense. Its clergy "suffer" misinterpretation, misunderstanding, and rejection from their people and see themselves as martyrs. Indeed, they thrive on the sense that they live rejection of people seeing in it a reflection of the suffering servant.

But the whole thing has become perverted and warped. Jesus suffered as a result of his life of service and challenge to authorities. He did not "see himself" as a "suffering servant"—he suffered because his servanthood was opposed. **His mission itself was the active one of ministry, not the resultant one of being persecuted and made to suffer.** The cross is not the summary of the

© 1969 Abingdon Press

gospel: it is the sign of the gospel's rejection by men. The Christians must live out the *whole* gospel, which means acting as if the whole Jesus story, the Jesus thing, was now happening still in history. This is what "faith" is for. Not "believing that Jesus died for me" (which may or may not be useful or meaningful), but rather "believing that the Jesus thing is alive for me."

The Jesus thing, which is "ultimate," is thus the dynamic at work in the world. This has two implications.

First, as I have tried to show, the basic gospel story is about a hidden dynamic now at work everywhere. The *incarnation* means that the human scene hides the ultimate, that humanity is "divinity." Christ's *healing ministry* means that everyman becomes significant when he engages in healing; but this is not a matter of consciously finding a neighbor and doing good to him, but rather losing myself in a vocation in which I cease to consider myself and my neighbor at all. *The parables* describe not how good deeds become part of the Kingdom, but how all kinds of good and bad deeds are revealed as ways of dealing with God's real agenda, the wholeness of the secular. *Acted parables* are the imaginative "trick" whereby reconciliation or wholeness or acceptance is achieved, a "trick" being worked all the time by all men everywhere, if they in fact live as if their neighbor were other than he is, and as if they were themselves also other than they are. *Discipleship* is the secret discipline necessary to those who wish intentionally to engage in the secret action and dynamic which is salvation for all (though there are those who are disciples unintentionally, who do the deeds of Christ but who "follow not us").

The cross is the way of vicariousness whereby all men may bring blessing to all men. The *resurrection* is the acceptance that in fact rests on all men's engagement in the Christ dynamic. The *parousia* is the universalization and finalization of the Jesus dynamic as that which ultimately matters and will be seen to matter.

Secondly, it is important to see *the whole Jesus pattern* as the way of wholeness and significance, and not just parts of it.

At times, obviously, a single element in the Jesus story will make sense, will come alive, will become the dynamic for new actions, attitudes, or expectations. But just to go for one single action may lead one into oversimplification, or disappointment, or pride. For, just as the cross is meaningless and false on its own, so is every other element. But as a whole, all elements together create a new life story, a new vocation, as well as a new life-style, for the disciple.

Thus, every Jesus story begins with *incarnation*—getting where people are, living with them, sharing their lot. It goes on to *healing ministry*—listening to what people's real needs are, being the patient washer of feet or cleaner of streets or brewer of tea. It then with love and care, not breaking the bruised reed, will seek to lift out into the light that points, people, groups, happenings, which bring love, healing, acceptance, or significance: the ministry of *parables*. Then perhaps there will be specific actions: not great actions, but small, meaningful, planned, strategic actions, which are *acted parables,* prophetic signs, imaginative instances, which can liberate old elements in the situation and hold up new possibilities. But all this will throw up and confirm the *disciple group;* it will force them together, and necessitate a discipline and a corporate mutual reliance. And perhaps there will be "polarization," conflict, the parting of the ways, new alliances with strange bedfellows: *the cross.* And the cross is also the loneliness of the vicarious initiator, who "does his thing" because it is "everybody's." Then, finally, there might be signs of *resurrection,* as the deed catches on, or the new style evokes response, or the group is thrilled with a momentary success, or the disciple experiences "the joy of the resurrection." And occasionally, within the battles of history, he sees the *parousia,* the ultimate triumph of "the way."

I believe that this theology *is* Christianity. Thus, I believe that it is what the churches should be embodying in their life in the future. Clearly, aspects of it have influenced churches in the past at various times; clearly, they do so now. But to attempt to redesign the whole resources of Christendom around this theological agenda would take more time than we have: though there are agencies where these agendas—or others very like them—are being pursued.[2]

At present, I believe that this kind of theology operates mainly in small groups. Part Four is thus concerned with one small experimental group—the Ashram Community. Its story is worth telling here for three reasons: First, because it has derived its life and ethos from the same groups within which the theology just described has emerged. Secondly, because it is typical of many para-church groups, but has probably taken the need for self-discovery, self-description, and self-discipline more seriously. Thirdly, because "the Jesus thing" remains just another theological toy without some indication of where it leads to.

[2] See, e.g., the Report, *Ministry in Cities,* and my article, "Playing God for the City," both in *New City* 3 (Summer, 1972). Also an earlier attempt, "A Church for the Metropolis," in *Here I Stand* (London: Epworth Press, 1967), pp. 69-79—a volume in many respects indicating the need for radicalism in the churches' present thinking.

AN EXPERIMENTAL COMMUNITY

A CELEBRATION OF ASHRAM COMMUNITY

O sing unto the Lord a new song for he has done marvelous things,
For even in this small house, among this struggling remnant,
Is living water for a thirsting world.

Leader: We give thanks for Ashram Community
Not because its church is a great building,
But because it is a pilgrim people
That has come to the city of need.

Response: Hallelujah and Amen we have come this far,
We seek the next step of the way.

Leader: We give thanks when we come to Ashram House
And tell the children we are coming to church
And they say, "What, is this a church?"
And we are forced to clarify new visions
And put our faith to the test.

Response: Hallelujah and Amen we have come this far,
We seek the next step of the way.

O sing unto the Lord a new song for he has done marvelous things,
For even in this small house, among this struggling remnant,
Is living water for a thirsting world.

Leader: We give thanks for Ashram Community
For throwing out the husks of religiosity
And seeking the kernel of Christ;
For its faith in the infinite diversity of people,
And its evoking of each person's very own gifts.

Response: Hallelujah and Amen we have come this far,
We seek the next step of the way.

Leader: We give thinks for Ashram Community
For its welcome to foreigners from other countries
(Even crazy Americans and beautiful tall Vikings).
For its welcome to the alienated, wherever they come from,
Around the corner, out of the university, from dead church
Or smug neighborhoods that have closed themselves to
    hurt.
Its welcome says, not here is a place,
But here is a way—we trust you as a traveling companion,
We dare to risk the future with you.

Response: Hallelujah and Amen we have come this far,
We seek the next step of the way.

Ralph and Julia Ketcham
(Syracuse, New York)
Sheffield Agape, May, 1972

THE BEGINNINGS OF ASHRAM COMMUNITY

On the fourth of March, 1967, I had a meal in Manchester with four lay friends in their twenties—John Wood, David Parish, Peter Crompton, and Dickson Pope. They came from different situations in and around Manchester. They had one thing in common: general frustration all around at what the church was and was doing. "Ideas which work elsewhere never work in the local church"; "a frustrating lack of ecumenical activity"; "the church is not prepared to be worried about the things I am worried about"; "they will not change—all they're concerned about is 'getting the people in'—which never comes off"; "the church I go to won't consider stewardship, or the steward will resign"; "the only thing I've been asked to do is lead a group of eighty-year-olds."

So, joined by a few others, we called a weekend conference which we entitled, "Living and Surviving in Methodism Today." Thirty-six came from many parts of the country. There were no set speeches and no visiting speakers, but the themes for each open session revealed a wide variety of need, frustration, disappointment, and determination to provide some means whereby Methodists "on their beam ends" could be helped to remain in the church and in Christian faith. Faced with a situation in which there seemed to be isolated Methodists all over the country who derived little or nothing from the local life of their churches, the Conference set its mind to the discovery of means whereby the individual at least could be held and encouraged to grow.

Thus, the early sessions on "Where I Am Now," and "Whence Do I Receive" led on to a study of "A Contemporary Style of Life," and of some disciplines which existed outside Methodism. Finally, four groups worked on various aspects of the question, "What Can We Do for One Another?" and the skeleton of a pattern emerged. The members present finally pledged themselves to:

1. *A Minimum Devotional Discipline.* Initially, this was decided to be the reading of three selected books, with discussion on them at local or regional meetings. Later, agreed reading of books of the Bible was suggested (not a daily lectionary).

2. *The Formation of Small Groups in Localities.* These would come together between individuals in circuits or groups of churches with a fourfold aim of common discipline to study, devotion, work in the community, and enjoyment.

3. *Periodic Regional "Ashram" Weekends (residential).* These would be open to all who felt the need of them, but some would be obligatory on those committed to the movement. Similar weekend or quarterly day gatherings would also provide meeting points and action sources for members.

4. *A Rule of Life.* This would require much experiment and mutual frankness, but it was felt that one of the problems of many people in the church was that the only standards of behavior put forward were irrelevant, and consequently there was no discipline. Specific points of "involvement" would be part of any rule.

Hendrik Kramer says that "the ashram usually combines the Indian idea of retreat for the cultivation of spiritual life and religious study with the European idea of a settlement for service to the environment in various ways." This, it was felt, was so near to what those present desired to provide for, that the name Ashram was chosen and has stuck.

Quarterly Ashram meetings have been held ever since, with one or more yearly weekends together. Of the four items mentioned above, the devotional discipline has varied in usefulness and in existence. Small groups have met informally in localities, but the quarterly Day Ashram gathering has been a central feature, and still is. The rule of life has been furthered spasmodically by those who felt called specifically to it.

All the usual "renewal" concerns were constantly studied, and pilot projects worked out. World poverty, politics, acted parables, church reform, and personal vocation were constantly discussed and acted upon. Two actions were of special significance.

First, Ashram became associated with Merfyn Temple's concern to get teams of committed and trained laypeople working with the poor in Zambia. Ashram produced, in 1968, the first appeal for a Day's Pay to support this, and has continued with this discipline, although the whole Methodist Church was asked to support a similar discipline on behalf of world poverty in 1969. The original statement in the leaflet labeled "Attack" is perhaps worth recording:

How can public opinion be changed?
Christians believe in the method of the sign, the prophetic action, the "acted parable"—the method whereby they first embody and put into practice a truth or a policy which ultimately must be taken up by everyone—politicians included. There are two sides to this "sign" of identification with the poor.
1—It must be something relevant to them—attacking the root causes of poverty in a way determined by them.
—Hence Technical Teams for Rural Advance.
2—It must be something relevant to us—that is, effort within our capacity, but significant enough to make a real claim on us, as a "First Fruit" of our commitment.
—Hence a Day's Wages.

Altogether, £1,500 (*ca.* $3,750) has been raised through the Day's Wages of a small group of people, and while Merfyn Temple felt in the end that our "acted parable" had done its job and helped precipitate the whole church into action, yet the discipline continues, each Lent a Day's Wage being given to selected projects.

The second action that came out of Ashram community was the decision to set up community houses. This is the subject of two later chapters.

One of the great dangers in any kind of para-church organization is that it becomes "institutionalized." But "institutional-

photo by Bracey Holt

ization" as a disease is a matter of degree. During 1971-72, we discovered that we were running up large private debts in order to do what the whole community decided. We had no resources to back up new branches or new houses. So at the A.G.M. in June, 1972, we wrote around to everyone on our lists in these terms:

Some people feel they need to put their money into the things they believe in. And we all need to have confidence in what we are doing, and this is the result of having at least enough to act when we need to act. We must will the means, as well as choose the ends. Our ambitions and ideals demand commitment, and we know the problem of asking people for serious commitment. Only when people know what you want to do with the money, will they pay. But we cannot do anything without the money, which means people paying first. We believe there is now sufficient confidence in what we have done and plan to do, and in what we stand for, to make a serious commitment justified.

We now have three kinds of membership—honorary members, who give £25 to committees of forty; this lasts 3 years; ordinary members, who pay the annual subscription of a minimum of £2; and pledged members, who make an annual pledged commitment of at least 1 percent of yearly income, after tax and insurance deductions. Money is allocated on a proportionate basis agreed by the A.G.M. The tri-annual journal, ACT, which also commenced in 1972, keeps the 150 members in touch, and provides a mailing list service for the increasing number of people interested in the community or considering membership.[1]

THE ASHRAM COMMUNITY "ETHOS"

At the fourth annual residential conference, held at Cliff Conference Centre, Calver, December 10-12, 1971, some of the 50 members present tried to set down their own "definitions" of the community. The results indicate both the pluralism that is bound to exist where a group of strong-minded individuals do anything, and also a common ethos which had formed over those four years. "Form critics" may imagine who wrote which: they vary from the mundane and practical to the idealistic and prophetic.

The Ashram Community is a group of people seeking to affirm that there is still hope in the way of Jesus.

The Ashram Community are people, who, although their theology ranges from traditional to radical, have found it necessary to come together in order that they can "live" Jesus in their lives, through mutual study, discussion, worship and action.

The Ashram Community is a group of people who seek together to work out a Christian life style relevant for today's world, involving suitable forms of discipleship, commitment and activity.

The Ashram Community is a group of people attempting to find life styles, ways of worship and mutual help which are for them the

---

[1] The Ashram Community journal, ACT, is published in February, June, and October—annually (Ashram Community Office, 239 Abbeyfield Road, Sheffield S4 7AW).

expression of response to Jesus Christ in the situation today.

The Ashram Community is a group who no longer see the institutional Church to be doing the Jesus thing, except marginally here and there, and who are searching to bring together meaningful units of people who can "be the Body of Christ" in a thoroughly secular way. They will be concerned to (1) Get on with some Jesus actions, (2) Develop new forms of mutual inspiration and stimulation, (3) Provide a place where many in the no-man's land of the fringes of the Church can be built up and held together, and (4) Continually analyze and probe the theological basis of what they do.

The Ashram Community is (1) The only Christian alternative for today's Church, (2) Tomorrow's Church in today's times, (3) The living Church within the community, (4) The Christian base for experimental witness within the community and (5) Christ through man serving and man through Christ in direct outreach.

From these and several other "definitions" which were also written it seems to me that six common elements clearly emerge:

1. *The Figure of Jesus*—whether as author, pattern, model, initiator, or inspiration.

2. *The Jesus Thing*—the way, style, technique, happening, which is what Jesus embodies and points to.

3. *A Style of Life*—attempts at meaningful secular discipleship, and relevant forms of personal and corporate discipline.

4. *A Constant Quest*—for new understandings of the Jesus thing for the sake of the future; a willingness, even, to be a guinea pig for tomorrow's church; a determination perpetually to examine actions and presuppositions in the light of theology and of experience.

5. *A Common Action*—in community, politics, society, in specific local situations or "crunch" issues.

6. *Mutual Help*—through a reliance on one another in human caring, judgment, discussion, study, vocation, and through commitment to specific people in small groups, in community houses, or in cells.

On two points—vital ones—the members of the community are

not agreed. Indeed, the very fact that disunity on these two points is tolerable within a community of such ethos and commitment is itself striking. It indicates, not that the two matters are unimportant, but that the other elements—the figure of Jesus, the Jesus thing, the style of life, etc.—are more important. It indicates the way in which a contemporary community can and does go far beyond the more traditional aspects of experimental community life.

The two points are Belief in God, and Church Allegiance.

Belief in God. Some members regard Christianity as a spiritual religion, think of God as a personal supernatural Being, and view future life as a possibility or a certainty. Other members, probably a growing number, see these as irrelevant to varying degrees, and as matters of opinion which do not vitally affect much of their own and the community's life. Others, again, see all belief in the supernatural, or in God as a person, or in immortality, as a positive obstacle to reliance in faith upon Jesus and the Jesus thing.

Church Allegiance. Some members see continuing membership in existing Christian denominations as a necessary and vital part of their discipleship and obedience to Christ. Others, probably again a growing number, regard adherence to traditional churches as a necessary evil or a possible good, but not as the absolutely essential implication of belonging to the community. Others, finally, see Ashram community as for them the only possible Christian community, which wholly replaces the old churches as source of inspiration, guidance, help, correction, and discipline.

We are only just beginning to realize what all this means to us in the life of the community—and, indeed, what it means for us personally. But several implications become possible.

1. *Essentials Emerge Along the Way.* We did not know before we began, what were going to be the essentials of our life together. We do not know now what the essentials may be in five years, or even two. There is a commitment which is prior to knowing anything to which one is committed—a style, ethos, way. This seems to be at present the only "essential."

2. *Pluralism Applies to Everything Else.* Each man is not his

own priest, but each man is his brother's priest, which means that he must welcome and support that form of faith and commitment which is actually working in and for his brother. Thus, pluralism must apply within the community, just as the church as a whole outside the community must learn to welcome pluralism, and the community as part of that pluralism.

3. *Care Must Be Taken to Avoid Offense.* Obviously, those who do not think of a personal, addressable deity are not going to "switch off" every time a prayer is said in traditional Thou or You form. But increasingly the effort will be made to speak so that all are edified, and none made to stumble or be confused.

4. *The Community Must Increasingly Act as Church.* If there are even only a few to whom Ashram community is the only Christian church, then the community must devise aspects of its life which take account of this. It must provide regular worship. It must provide sustaining pastoral care. It must organize its finances so that people can make regular stewardship gifts to it. It must not, however, become a denomination, even though it cannot avoid being an "order" within the whole catholic church.

5. *The Jesus Action Must Determine All Else.* We only find ourselves now where we are because of being led by what seemed

to us implications of the Jesus way. **So we must in the future allow only those things to remain which then are still relevant to what then appears as the Jesus way.** Christology must dominate organization. The Spirit must constantly crush and reform the old, or create the totally new.

THE AGAPE

For a long period we discussed the question of regular monthly services of worship for Ashram community members and others. We held back because we did not want to be seen to be putting on rival services, which might become alternatives to the ordinary churches' services. But the community in and around Ashram House is becoming a "mini-ecclesia," and in the end has to think not only for itself but also for the fringe Christians, inquiring agnostics, and "lost" churchgoers, who are looking for some place where they can engage in some meaningful, corporate act centered on the Jesus thing without being tied to old forms and concepts.

So, in December, 1971, we decided to go ahead with Agapes in our Community Houses or wherever else there seemed a need or a demand.

We chose to call our gathering together an Agape, because this has a long history in the church but has fallen into disuse. It also seemed to us a far richer and more meaningful way of pointing to the Jesus thing and the Jesus action, than the Holy Communion or Eucharist. In any case, the latter is still the bone of contention within the churches, and it was not our wish to take over unnecessary controversy from past centuries into our simple rites.

Agape is the New Testament word for self-giving love. *Eucharist* is the New Testament word for thanksgiving celebration. In Christian history, *Agape* has come to be used of "love-feasts," informal meals, and times of togetherness and mutual sharing; and *Eucharist* is used of the church's sacrament of Holy Communion.

In this simple service, we celebrate a "love-feast" and find it to be a "holy communion." We set the bread and the cup of Christ within the context of a real symbolic meal, which itself is set in a community of concern and commitment represented by each one who is there. We set our meal, in imagination, in the time of Christ's earthly ministry, when he invited all to share his feast.

Friends sit around a low, central table. A front living room serves well, with as many on the carpet as in armchairs. People take what part they are asked to. A "leader" keeps a semblance of order . . .

PART ONE—THE AGAPE MEAL

Informal Sing-In

Songs or hymns are sung quietly as people assemble.

Introduction

The leader briefly welcomes people and explains what will happen. *Then all say together:*

> Now the times are filled full,
> Now is the day of wholeness,
> Now God's place is within humanity.

Leader: Now the time of your liberation has arrived,
Now is the celebration of the Kingdom.
All join in the Lord's Prayer.

Personal Introduction

At this point the leader introduces himself/herself to everyone, and shakes hands with the person sitting on his or her left, who then introduces himself/herself and shakes hands with his or her neighbor, and so on around the room.

The Table Is Set

Someone places a candle on the table and says:
> Jesus Christ, the Light of the world.

Someone places the food on the table and says:
> Jesus Christ, the Life of the world.

Someone places the drink on the table and says:
> Jesus Christ, the Living Water.

Someone places a cross on the table and says:
> Jesus Christ, the Way, the Truth, and the Life.

Feeding the People

Someone reads the story of Jesus feeding the five thousand (Luke 9: 10-17).

The Agape

The leader presents the food and says:
> Jesus Christ is the Bread of Life.

The leader presents the drink and says:
> Jesus Christ is the Living Water.

The food is then passed around the room from person to person, each one saying:

Christ is the Bread of Life.
The drink is then passed around the room, each one saying:
Christ is the Living Water.
(After this, the children who wish can go out to another room.)

PART TWO—ELEMENTS OF COMMUNITY WORSHIP

Communal Sermon

Someone reads a passage from scripture or other book, and asks:
What does this say to us, here and now?
The leader and all present respond as they will.
A song or hymn could be sung at this point.

Sharing of Concerns

People mention things going on in the world, the city, the neighborhood, group, community, or family.
There is a silence between each concern, during which people can think about them, or pray.

Common Confession

Someone says:
Let us examine ourselves because we want to go on trying to live the community of Christ which demands us to be wholly free.
All now respond together:
We confess our failing in community,
Our lack of understanding,
Our lack of forgiveness,
Our lack of openness,
Our lack of sensitivity.
We confess the times
When we are too eager to be better than others,
When we are too rushed to care,
When we are too tired to bother,
When we are too lazy really to listen,
When we are too quick to act from motives other
than love.

(Silence for self-realization.)

Then all say together:
>   Brothers, we forgive,
>   We trust that we are forgiven.

Affirmation

The Agape concludes with all saying together:
>   Christ is not dead,
>   Christ is bread,
>   Christ is light,
>   Christ is the Way,
>   The Way for moving,
>   The Truth for grasping,
>   The Life for living.
>   Christ's people are alive,
>   Trying to be leaven,
>   Trying to be light,
>   Trying to be the Way,
>   The Way for moving,
>   The Truth for grasping,
>   The Life for living.
>   Through Jesus we live,
>   Through Jesus we love,
>   Jesus in words,
>   Jesus in deeds,
>   Jesus in action.
>   Jesus,
>   The Way, the Truth, and the Life.

THE HOUSEWARMING

Clearly, the para-church is more at home when it is in homes or houses than when it is in a church building. Elaborate ritual surrounds every temple, cathedral, chapel, or religious meeting-house. No ritual surrounds the home. Yet it is in the home, be it the home of the ordinary Ashram community member, or the community house for those who live there, that most of the "Jesus Things" will be done, or talked about, or prayed over. So it is natural that a "Housewarming Liturgy" should be used, initially for the community houses, but also now, in whole or part, for anyone who wants to "bless" the place where he or she will dwell, as a roof over the mysteries of Christ-life.

The Ashram "Housewarming Liturgy" was written mainly by Chris Blackwell, and was first used by the Rochdale branch members and residents on the fifth of January, 1970. It was used for the Sheffield house on the fourth of December, 1971, and has also been used in other situations.

Chris argues in an article in *Act 2* that worship is "Thinking about life, before God." He sees four elements:

1. Worship must combine the flexibility and freedom which enables lively congregational participation, with definite words and actions which give the worship shape and purpose. Free (e.g., Methodist) worship is often *more* stereotyped than more catholic orders. 2. Worship cannot be all words: things to do, and things to see, touch (even eat) are vital. These non-verbal components of worship have become even more vital to communication in the age of the film, television, and poster advertising; and the R.C.s have the edge on the Free Churches every time here. 3. "Adoration" of God and "confession" of one's own failings cannot be meaningful unless related to Jesus— the model of True God, and the model of True Man. 4. **To "think about life, before God" is very different from thinking about God instead of life (which has been a traditional approach to worship).**

photo by Sid Dorris

You can see these four ideas worked out in the Housewarming Liturgy which follows: 1. The Liturgy is *put down on paper* for everyone involved to have before him as a pattern; but it permits a variety of performance. (A better example of this is the Church of South India's Communion Service, which lists two or three alternative sections at each stage of the order.) So there is structure, but also participation. 2. There is plenty of *non-verbal content:* four objects (a cross, a brick, a map, and a constitution) are brought up to the Worship center. There are silences for people to "do their own thing" in. 3. The *adoration/confession* is based on an outline of the person of Jesus, and response to this. 4. The *"thinking about life"* develops from the "imitation of Jesus," to think about what an Ashram House is all about, to say the "our Brother" which addresses the here-and-now, to pray about the life-setting of those present, and to meditate.

The Housewarming Liturgy begins with a period of silence, during which people reflect on a passage for meditation.

A HOUSEWARMING LITURGY

For Meditation

Come to the Lord, the living stone rejected as worthless by men, but chosen as valuable by God. Come as living stones, and let yourselves be used in building the spiritual temple, where you will serve as holy priests, to offer spiritual and acceptable sacrifices to God through Jesus Christ. For the scripture says:

"I chose a valuable stone

Which I now place as the cornerstone in Zion;

And whoever believes in him will never be disappointed."

This stone is of great value for you who believe; but for those who do not believe:

"The stone which the builders rejected as worthless

Turned out to be the most important stone."

And another scripture says,

"This is the stone that will make men stumble,

The rock that will make them fall."

They stumbled because they did not believe in the word; such was God's will for them.

But you are the chosen race, the King's priests, the holy nation, God's own people, chosen to proclaim the wonderful acts of God, who called you from the darkness into his own marvelous light. At one time you were not God's people, but now you are his people; at one time you did not know God's mercy, but now you have received his mercy.

I Peter 2:4-9 TEV

Preparation

Leader: In the Name of Jesus—
All: Incarnate, Crucified, and Living;
Yesterday, Today, and Tomorrow.
Leader: And before God—
All: Who sees what is done in secret,
And knows our needs before we ask. Amen.
Silence for preparation

The Past

Leader: Let us reflect on Jesus, the Word made flesh; and in Adoring the Father, let us also reflect on our failure to "attain to mature manhood, measured by nothing less than the full stature of Christ. . . ."
Let us celebrate Christ, and examine ourselves, in his presence. Father, to look at Christ is to realize our many failings: Christ was patient—always ready to listen—always ready to talk:
All: Lord, teach us to be patient.
Leader: Christ was at home everywhere, with everyone—including the lepers of society:
All: Lord, help us to be open to all.
Leader: Christ was not misled by labels or slogans—he met people:
All: Lord, help us to meet the reality behind the idea, the person behind the mask.
Leader: Christ was the incarnation of love—he gave himself:
All: Lord, help us to live for others.

Leader: Christ preached what he lived:
All: Lord, may our deeds speak.
Leader: Christ carried no grudges—forgives us all:
All: Lord, forgive us, and teach us to forgive.
Leader: Christ suffered and died for the world:
All: Lord, give us the courage to commit ourselves to life for mankind.
We ask this in Christ's Name. Amen.

Silence for private Confession and Thanksgiving.

Christ Is Present

A cross is placed centrally, and the bearer says:
The symbol of Christ's presence in the midst of his disciples, in the world, and particularly in this and every home. Jesus says: "Even the Son of Man did not come to be served but to serve, and to surrender his life as a ransom for many."
All: Be present, Lord Jesus Christ.
A brick is placed centrally, and the bearer says:
A symbol of the fabric and furnishings of this house. Peter says: "So come to him, our Living Stone—the stone rejected by men but choice and precious in the sight of God."
All: We pledge ourselves to maintain this house as a base for the on-going ministry of Christ.
A map of the city or neighborhood is placed centrally, and the bearer says:
A symbol of the people we seek to serve. Jesus says: "I tell you this: anything you do for one of my brothers here, however humble, you do for me."
All: We pledge ourselves to serve these people to the best of our ability, in the knowledge that in our neighborhood we meet and serve Christ.
The Constitution of the Ashram Trust is placed centrally, and the bearer says:
A symbol of the people actively and representatively involved in this project. Jesus says: "As the Father has sent me into the world, so I send you into the world."
All: Hands of Jesus, bless us. Feet of Jesus, lead us. Arms of Jesus,

uphold us. Heart of Jesus, burn in us. Presence of Jesus, be in our neighbor.

The "Our Brother"

(An adaptation of the "Our Father," based on Jesus' teaching that God and God's Kingdom are in one's brother.)
All say together:
Our brothers, alongside whom we live in the world, we want to love you as our very selves. We want the Kingdom of heaven to be yours, beginning here and now. We would serve you now and into eternity. We want all people to share fairly the riches of this world, today and everyday. Our brothers, we forgive whatever wrongs you may have done us; please forgive us the wrongs we have done you. Do not lean on us too heavily, our brothers; but when you must lean, let us lean on you, too. For God has committed to us the kingdom of faith, the power of hope, and the glory of love, for ever and ever. Amen.

At this point the present residents introduce themselves.

The Future

Leader: Let us pray for others, and for ourselves in the service of others—
Silence for private Intercession and Petition, or biddings for Prayer.
Leader: We offer . . .
All: We offer and present to you, O Lord, ourselves, our minds and bodies, to be a reasonable, holy, and living sacrifice to you.
Leader: Go in peace:
All: In the Name of Christ.
Leader: Amen.
All: Amen.

AN ASHRAM "CELL"

How are we to develop relevant forms of "community" for those who are unable to live in a community house, but who yet feel the compulsion to create a relevant form for themselves?

This is a question which, of course, has been with the church all through the ages, creating the "third orders" of laity connected with the great monastic orders, creating the "class meetings" of the early Methodists, creating movements like House Groups, Servants of Christ the King, Iona Community, the Taizé Community Assemblies, etc. Ashram Community cells take their place as one more effort in this direction, significant only because it began in the nineteen-seventies, with people who were looking for something arising out of their own history and ethos.

Thus Gwen Green summarized the findings of the working group that finally set us off on the "Cell":

An Ashram Cell is a group of people who meet to work out for themselves suitable forms of discipleship and common life.

The initial commitment involves two or three Ashram members getting together a small group, and meeting for three evenings to develop their own minimal discipline, including some form of commitment to stay together over a stated period. We report back to other Cells as decided.

The agenda of a Cell are settled by the group itself. The following are listed merely as possible ways in which a Cell might develop:

1. *Periods of being together* could be:

a) Meals, b) Days, c) Weekends.

2. *Aspects of Commitment* could be:

a) Finance, b) Time: work, leisure, family, service, c) Projects, d) Prayer and Devotion, e) Service in neighborhood.

3. *The Area of membership* could be from:

a) Parish or congregation, b) Ecumenical within a neighborhood, c) Likeminded people within a town or area.

In addition to Cells of this more disciplined kind, Ashram community members have, like many other Christians today, been involved in the rise of informal groups of marginal or post-Christians. The following description is by Kathleen Kinder and concerns a group in Settle, Yorkshire.

Our particular group was originally convened by my husband and me. The inspiration came out of the Methodist Ashram to which we belong. We asked to the first meeting people we knew who were in despair with the institutional church (Methodist, in the first instance), but who were convinced that the essence of the gospel was worth hanging on to.

After several meetings since March 1969 with Tony Wesson, we now have a membership of around 25; Anglicans, Methodists, Roman Catholics, and Quakers. More than half the group attend church infrequently. A good half (mostly Methodists) would describe their affiliation as nominal. One or two describe themselves privately as agnostic. We have teachers, civil servants, a social worker, an industrial physicist, a veterinary surgeon, housewives, a journalist, a secretary, a retired railwayman among our members. A Methodist minister from a neighboring circuit has recently asked to join. Less than half would claim they were intellectuals; the rest would be horrified by the description. Some had never met before the group convened. Most of us are in the 30-45 age-group.

Under Tony Wesson's expert guidance, we found a common identity and decided unanimously to accept the suggestion of a group member to study, and act on as far as we could, the root causes of world poverty.

This Settle group has now been going on long enough for it to be in a position to reflect on the significance of what it is doing. Kathleen Kinder's further comments on the group as a "mini-congregation" or "para-church" are therefore important:

1. We are more than a study-action group. We are a therapeutic agency for people who need to talk to help themselves. Any facilities that the organizational church may offer in this direction will be rejected by people who choose, by conviction, to remain outside. Mutual trust is the only foundation for the kind of fellowship the group provides.

2. We are finding a pastoral concern among ourselves. Two cases spring to mind: a Roman Catholic's "crisis of conscience" shared with a Methodist member, and only this week an agonizing marital problem shared with three other members of the group. The person concerned never dreamt of going to the minister of the church of which she is a nominal member.

3. We have no shadow of a doubt that we are evangelists, and make

no secret of the fact that one of our tasks is to persuade those who do the deeds of Christ "to name the Name." So far, we have no act of worship, but it is dawning on some that we may reach a point in our fellowship when we decide spontaneously to offer a simple act of worship, of intercession, of thanksgiving, the breaking of bread maybe. One reason why church worship has gone dead for many is that it is no longer a communal act done spontaneously by people committed to one another.

A Rochdale District Ashram Community Day. Standing: Chris Blackwell. Seated (from left to right): James, John, Christopher, and Grace Vincent, and Kathleen Kinder.

4. The tension is increasing for those of us committed to the organizational church. My husband and I halved our preaching appointments. The concerns of the group are more real and therefore more important than taking services in empty chapels. In this largely Conservative-Evangelical circuit, "Radical" is a dirty word, and we face hostility nearly every time in circuit and church meetings.

However, it has occurred to some of the group that we already bear a striking similarity to the early Methodist fellowships. We pray that we may succeed where they failed, and stay in the institutional church.

I can only add that this is becoming a decisive question for more and more such groups, all over the world. We must hope that Ashram Community, and similar organizations, can hold them in some kind of living contact with other Christians.

LIFE IN A COMMUNITY HOUSE

The Community House as a form of the church is not a new idea. Initially, in 1968, we were considerably helped by visits to and discussions with other houses, especially the Brotherhood of Prayer and Action, an Anglican "order," operating from a variety of houses and other bases, in Wolverhampton.

Since then, the distinctive lines of our own "houses" have emerged. Our houses are "owned" by the Ashram Community Trust, a registered charity. The management committee of the Trust (appointed by all community members) takes general responsibility and appoints four local trustees, who form a "house committee" with the residents and a few other local Ashram members. The size of house we look for would depend on the area; but both Rochdale and Sheffield houses can take up to eight residents, and this has been found to be a good number. Larger or smaller houses would comprise no problem. We have not yet been given a house for nothing, and even if we were, we would still want a group of committed local people prepared to put money and labor into getting it ready and standing by it. Accordingly, the local Ashram community branch forms a "Committee of Forty" consisting of people who will give £25 each to buying and equipping a house.

There has been within the community considerable discussion on how we should describe the purpose of the houses. The following was worked out early in 1972 and is used as a basic statement for discussion among ourselves and as a rough description of our ethos, for people interested.

1. *An Ashram Community House* is a place where members of the Ashram community, who see their present vocation in this way, live and work together in a residential community.

2. *The ethos of an Ashram Community House* is thus the ethos of the Ashram community. It is avowedly and openly Christian. All shades of Christian belief and denomination are welcome,

although the main leadership and membership of the community is radical Christian.

3. *The first purpose of an Ashram Community House* is to form a para-church, a "frontier" mini-ekklesia, a neighborhood or even street congregation. It is also a "home" for radical Christians in a wider area. This shows itself in:

a) *Internal Life.* The house residents share devotions over the common evening meal at 6; have a monthly residents' fellowship with a local Ashram community ministerial adviser; take periodic day retreats; and share in communal finance.

b) *Provision for Others.* The house entertains, and organizes with other local Ashram members, the monthly Agape, and other fellowship as needed, e.g., radical Bible study. It also acts as host to local youth groups, holds weekend conferences for interested visitors, and acts as a focus for local branch concerns.

4. *The second purpose of an Ashram Community House* is to operate in the light of the ministries of Christ to those in need, "living Christ's life among the poor."

a) *Finding the Local Agenda.* The house must assimilate to the needs of the area and find out how best it can help, in order to be "neighbors."

b) *Theology-Action Study.* The house must discover what, in the Christian faith and dynamic, there is to be brought to the problems of the agenda.

5. *Location.* The criteria for locating an *Ashram Community House* are thus not simply areas of need, but areas within which the presence of a new-style Christian mini-community is called for. In fact, this can be anywhere, and probably should in the end be everywhere. Thus, the *Community House* is not a social work agency, but a new style for the disciples of Jesus, and is relevant everywhere. It is a "roof for the Jesus action."

6. *Management.* House affairs are in the hands of the house committee, consisting of residents, trustees, and other appointed local Ashram community members (e.g., trustees' wives), with the local trustees chairman as house chairman.

The people who form an *Ashram House* are in their twenties and thirties. They are usually people whose qualifications and previous posts would prepare them for better jobs and better living quarters than those in which they have banded together in an Ashram house, though "slumming it" is not the rule. They do not usually come from the city where the house is situated.

Our first three houses were opened in Rochdale (January, 1970), Sheffield (September, 1971), and Middlesbrough (Spring, 1973). All are in inner-city areas, so that the agenda of the inner-city has become our agenda.

In response to this, the house functions as a single household of concerned persons, seeking to be neighbors in a difficult environment. The members are not social workers, or evangelists, or political activators, but a family, which believes that their common life as a family can do something to release in themselves, corporately and individually, and in others around them, a genuine family concern for neighbors. They therefore welcome groups in which Ashram house members are individually involved. At Rochdale this has meant the Asian Boys' Club, the Rochdale Ashram Branch, the local Independent Councillor's consulting hours, the Committee Rooms for the Labor candidate during local elections, an occasional Social Workers Group, and a fortnightly Radical Bible Study. At Sheffield it has meant the Ashram House Advice Centre (organized by the house with the help of city official and voluntary agencies), the Nottingham Street Neighbourhood Group, the Sheffield Inner City Ecumenical Mission Social Care Working Party, the Urban Theology Unit, the Pitsmoor Action Group, and sundry youth and community action. Sheffield runs a Sunday evening "open house" for young people, Rochdale a monthly Saturday evening "open house" for anyone interested. The Sheffield house is a full member of the Sheffield Inner City Ecumenical Mission; the Rochdale house has traditional links especially with the Champness Hall (Rochdale Methodist Mission), but is now developing wider relations with Presbyterian, Anglican, and Methodist churches.

The special needs of the inner city, and the attraction and challenge of its varied and cosmopolitan character, will doubtless mean that other similar situations will arise in which houses are called for, as in Nottingham. But we are already talking about experimenting with community houses in a city center situation, in an upper-class suburb, and in a small town. In addition, we are also looking at a specific possibility of running a special project of some kind within a residential house—which would require full-time members caring for others in need who would also be resident. Finally, we are aware of the need to develop a small community where three or four families in single homes would live near one another.[1]

In the next chapter two of the first members in Rochdale and Sheffield, writing in January, 1972, describe some of the "signs of life" already appearing. The two other first residents in Rochdale, I should add, were Chris Blackwell and Elaine Peace.

SIGNS OF LIFE: ROCHDALE AND SHEFFIELD

TWO YEARS IN ASHRAM HOUSE, ROCHDALE
By GLADYS BRIERLEY

Picture a decaying street, houses derelict and rat-infested, or maintaining an air of diminishing respectability. Picture a group of dark-skinned men; women in colorful saris; children with dirty noses; mini-skirted teen-agers pushing prams; a bent and elderly woman creeping unnoticed, as a group of gesticulating Ukranians hurry by. Look at the neat net curtains and distinguish a frail hand holding one aside to allow a frail face a view of the street. Look at the net curtains next door, torn and dirty, barely hiding the misery within. Listen to the shrill voices, the guttural voices, the obscene words, the indecipherable words. Smell the chappatis and curry,

---

[1] For attractive surveys of contemporary community experiments, see two issues of *Risk:* Vol. 5, No. 3/4 (1969) on "Renewal," and Vol. 8, No. 1 (1972) on "All Things in Common" (Publication Office, World Council of Churches, 150 Rue de Ferney, Geneva 20, Switzerland). Also see the tri-annual journal, *Community,* obtainable from "One for Christian Renewal" (c/o 52 High Road, London N2 9PM).

Ashram House, Rochdale

fish and chips. Smell the fetid odor of rotting refuse, unwashed bodies, dirty nappies. Feel the grime on the gatepost, the rustle of leaves on the pavement where one brave tree sheds its autumn load. See the broken van on the corner, the smart new Viva opposite. Hear the ringing bell of the "black peas man."

You may be in any downtown urban area—you are, in fact, in King Street South, Rochdale. As the *News of the World* has it, "All human life is here," and so have *we* been here for two years now, sharing the life of this cosmopolitan community; trying to be a new community transplanted into an established one. For there is no doubt about it, that King Street South is a "community" in its own right. Our fears of rejection have proved groundless; we have been absorbed into its wide street, accepted by its residents, and have shared its many concerns.

The house has taken on a comfortable appearance. Shabby enough but still fair among its neighbors, number 17 is substantial and warm. Some decorating still needs doing, but the inside is bright and cheerful. The new electric bell on the white front door is husky from constant use.

We consented to "let the area write the agenda," and the practical way in which we have operated has emerged from living in the street and being responsive to its moods. Lest this should conjure up a picture of a "first-aid system," an ambulance waiting on the street corner, I must add that the calls on us have arisen as they would on any good neighbor, spontaneously and *ad hoc.* The difference is only that there are always three, four, six of us, consciously willed to deal with an emergency. And to help one another and to console when disappointment is uppermost.

I like to think of the house operating simultaneously in five different ways:

Communally, because we share a common hearth, money, time, and rely on one another for support;

Socially, as we find ourselves able to help our neighbors practically, providing material aid, use of the 'phone, and in countless familiar ways;

Pastorally, we have endeavored to keep a warm, open house

where all could come for "tea and sympathy"—or celebration. We have tried to offer a therapeutic group to friends;

Politically, as a neighborhood pressure group working with elected councillors (and there is need for a watchful eye in this area of change and redevelopment);

Theologically, by discussion groups, conferences, house church, etc.

Looking back over two years, I see I have gained greater clarity and insight into human values. I question my own and others' motives, and am not always satisfied with the answers. Are we really helping the "para-church," or are we just a bunch of "do-gooders"? Did Jesus intend no more than loving our neighbor? What is love? What about the political systems? What is sacrifice? Is it necessary? What does the church mean in this neighborhood? Do we speak of God in the context of filth and drug addiction? Does he care anyway? Could a humanist do what we are attempting, and do it better? Could the social agencies?

An Ashram Community Agape.

Perhaps I could answer the last one, and the answer would be "no." There is value in living in the same street, sharing the discomfort of a deprived neighborhood, and the inconvenience of an address the wrong side of town. It means identifying. Identifying with a warm community of people who perhaps have lost a little hope, expectancy, and zest for living. It means being thrilled by the recognition of "the other" in our unlikeliest brothers. It means an argument in a launderette, which identifies one with the Pakistani culture. It means rich relationships, chastening, humbling experiences. It means dirty kids' happy faces on the way home from the park. It means hours of agonizing over the imponderables, posing questions to which there are no answers.

FOUR MONTHS IN ASHRAM HOUSE, SHEFFIELD

By ROY CROWDER

Ashram House, 84 Andover Street, Pitsmoor, is an experiment in Christian Community. The main form of Christian witness today is the coming together of people for worship—a relatively large number of people for a relatively short period of time. However, over the centuries, many different forms of community have existed which have sought to express the gospel to men of their time.

Two things are happening in the latter half of the twentieth century which must make us wonder about the future of the church. First, the established way in which the church operates is failing. Here and there, congregations may increase, but overall they decrease. In the inner-city areas, churches of every denomination have been coming to the critical point when their decline in numbers makes them unable to finance large buildings. The fight for existence makes churches look inward for support, and increasingly the church becomes just another compartment in people's fragmented lives of work, sleep, sustenance, play, and human relations.

Secondly, all over the world young people are coming together

Ashram House, Pitsmoor

to form communes and communities. Some are ways of escaping from the pressures and evils of the world outside. Others are committed to changing society through political action or charitable action. Ashram community is a way of trying to rediscover the essential corporateness of Christianity in the modern world.

Ashram community, Pitsmoor, is a group of six people who have committed themselves to living, ministering, and worshiping together in an inner-city area. It does not see itself in conflict with the established churches, but rather as a unique facet of the overall witness of Christians. Above all, it seeks to be part of the neighborhood to which it ministers, and this will inevitably take time. Members of the Ashram community are involved at the moment in getting to know people and becoming an accepted part of the wider community. From this we hope that a deeper understanding of the needs of the area will be achieved. Already we have been involved in helping a number of people with personal needs and also have been taking initiative in the formation of a residents' group in the surrounding streets to liaise with the corporation whose development plan has recently been published. We hope that the House will become a natural focus for the neighborhood, and that the home atmosphere will provide the sort of ministry to the area which a congregation would not find possible.

The present residents are: Rita Norris, a teacher who has been living in Sheffield for two years now; Hilary Walker, who has recently taken a social work post in the city; Roy Crowder, a nurse at Middlewood Hospital; Ray Hinch, the ministerial assistant in the Sheffield Inner City Ecumenical Mission; Howard Knight, who is youth leader of the Brunswick Youth and Community Centre just down the road from the House; and Ian Laughton, who leads and drives the Grimesthorpe Playbus which provides preschool play facilities for children of the inner city.

Ashram community is open to the future. It is searching for new ways of being the church—that group of people committed to doing and pointing toward the deeds of Jesus in the world—new ways of worship, new ways of being a family. But it realizes that its roots lie in a long tradition of communal living right from the times of the first Christians. Above all, we are looking for new ways of bringing hope to those inner-city areas which are so much the product of despair and apathy.

Four of the first residents at Sheffield House, Christmas, 1971. Left to right, Ray Hinch, Rita Norris, Howard Knight, and Roy Crowder.

EPILOGUE

Living in the world today and being a part of the Church as the Body
of Christ is rather like living in a down-town improvement area.
I stand on a street corner.
I can tell that certain parts of the area are worth keeping and doing
up. But certain parts have just got to go.
So the bulldozers move in and the dust flies.
The acrid smoke of old mattresses and granny's wallpaper gets up my
nose.
And on a Sunday morning the men come in their lorry to take the
good bits away.
As for the Church:
I'm not sure whether the bulldozers have moved in yet or not.
There are a few men taking the good bits away.
And the smoke gets right up my nose.

> Peter Crompton,
> Rochdale House, Summer, 1972.

These lines describe an ethos, a way of looking at life, a way
of feeling about life, a style, a stance, an expectation, a commitment.

In our time, and perhaps for a time in the future, it is sufficient
and vital that there are people saying where they stand, how they
operate. And in a time of confusion in the world and the church,
we need to know that there are people actually making something
of the gospel story, and being driven, at least in places, to gear
their lives around what they can make of it.

Pluralism means that every Christ-man must do his own gospel thing. Catholicity means variety and richness. It means that everyone is "in." This is a time for catholicity. A new orthodoxy might emerge in the future.

John Robinson says that "the real denial of Christ is not that he

photo by Toge Fujihira

is not named, but that he is not represented." [1] The real glory of Christ in the flesh is that, whether he is named or not, he is in fact being represented—in private action, in small groups, in corporate action, within institutions, within the institutional churches, within the para-churches, within nations, within secular history, all over the world today. The world church today is

[1] John A. T. Robinson, *The Difference in Being a Christian Today* (Philadelphia: The Westminster Press, 1972), p. 43.

kept going, not by the administrators and financiers, but by the little pieces of incarnation, healing, parable, and community that keep appearing, despite us.

"The Jesus thing" wants simply to point to this. As a new slogan, it is useful to some, confusing to others. But it may serve to help us constantly question what is the gospel, and the gospel for us. Whenever we find a "place to stand," it is only for that "day," perhaps for that "age," but not more. What is vital and what is permanent is the actual life-giving dynamic, the "thing" itself, which Jesus is and points to, the Way, Truth, and Life within the world.

What is vital beyond that is that there should be people who seek out and live by it consciously, intentionally, committedly. As if the "thing" that moves and holds them is what "rolls the world along."

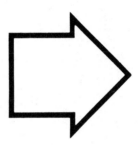

The Vincent Family: John, Christopher, James, Faith, and Grace.